FAITH

━━━ IN THE FACE OF ━━━

APOSTASY

T H E   G O S P E L   A C C O R D I N G   T O
T H E   O L D   T E S T A M E N T

A series of studies on the lives
of Old Testament characters, written for
laypeople and pastors, and designed to
encourage Christ-centered reading, teaching,
and preaching of the Old Testament.

TREMPER LONGMAN III
J. ALAN GROVES

Series Editors

FAITH

IN THE FACE OF

APOSTASY

THE GOSPEL ACCORDING TO
ELIJAH & ELISHA

RAYMOND B. DILLARD

P&R
P U B L I S H I N G
P.O. BOX 817 • PHILLIPSBURG • NEW JERSEY 08865-0817

Unless otherwise indicated, all Scripture quotations are from the HOLY BIBLE, NEW INTERNATIONAL VERSION®. NIV®. Copyright © 1973, 1978, 1984 by International Bible Society. Used by permission of Zondervan Publishing House. All rights reserved.

Page design by Tobias Design
Typesetting by Michelle Feaster

Printed in the United States of America

Library of Congress Cataloging-in-Publication Data

Dillard, Raymond B., d. 1993.
    Faith in the face of apostasy : the Gospel according to Elijah and Elisha / Raymond B. Dillard.
        p.   cm. — (The Gospel according to the Old Testament)
    Includes bibliographical references and index.
    ISBN 0-87552-650-0 (pbk.)
    1. Elijah (Biblical prophet) 2. Elisha (Biblical prophet)
3. Bible. O.T. Kings, 1st, XVII, 1-Kings, 2nd, XIII, 21-Criticism, interpretation, etc. 4. Bible. O.T. Kings, 1st, XVII, N.T.— Relation to Kings, 1st, XVII, 1-Kings, 2nd, XIII, 21.
    I. Title. II. Series.
BS580.E4D45 1999
222'.506—dc21   99–28026

This book is dedicated to

Rusty Anderson
Union Springs, Alabama

Jack Armstrong
Wilmington, Delaware

Brian Bankard
Baltimore, Maryland

—brothers who hear God's word
and put it into practice.
(Luke 8:21)

CONTENTS

FOREWORD

"The New Testament is in the Old concealed;
the Old Testament is in the New revealed."
—Augustine

Concerning this salvation, the prophets, who spoke of the grace that was to come to you, searched intently and with the greatest care, trying to find out the time and circumstances to which the Spirit of Christ in them was pointing when he predicted the sufferings of Christ and the glories that would follow. It was revealed to them that they were not serving themselves but you, when they spoke of the things that have now been told you by those who have preached the gospel to you by the Holy Spirit sent from heaven. Even angels long to look into these things. (1 Peter 1:10–12)

"In addition, some of our women amazed us. They went to the tomb early this morning but didn't find his body. They came and told us that they had seen a vision of angels, who said he was alive. Then some of our companions went to the tomb and found it just as the women had said, but him they did not see." He said to them, "How foolish you are, and how slow of heart to believe all that the prophets have spoken! Did not the Christ have to suffer these things and then enter his glory?" And beginning with Moses and all the Prophets, he explained to them what was said in all the Scriptures concerning himself. (Luke 24:22–27)

The prophets searched. Angels longed to see. And the disciples didn't understand. But Moses, the prophets, and all the Old Testament Scriptures had spoken about it— that Jesus would come, suffer, and then be glorified. God began to tell a story in the Old Testament, the ending for which the audience eagerly anticipated. But the Old Testament audience was left hanging. The plot was laid out but the climax was delayed. The unfinished story begged an ending. In Christ, God has provided the climax to the Old Testament story. Jesus did not arrive unannounced; his coming was declared *in advance* in the Old Testament, not just in explicit prophecies of the Messiah but by means of the stories of all of the events, characters, and circumstances in the Old Testament. God was telling a larger, overarching, unified story. From the account of creation in Genesis to the final stories of the return from exile, God progressively unfolded his plan of salvation. And the Old Testament account of that plan always pointed in some way to Christ.

AIMS OF THIS SERIES

The Gospel According to the Old Testament Series is committed to this proposition that the Bible, both Old and New Testaments, is a unified revelation of God, and that its thematic unity is found in Christ. The individual books of the Old Testament exhibit diverse genres and styles and individual theologies, but tying them all together is the constant foreshadowing and pointing to Christ. Believing in the fundamentally Christocentric nature of the Old Testament, as well as the New Testament, we offer this series of studies in the Old Testament with the following aims:

- to lay out the pervasiveness of the revelation of Christ in the Old Testament,
- to promote a Christ-centered reading of the Old Testament,
- to encourage Christ-centered preaching and teaching from the Old Testament.

To this end, the volumes in this series are written for pastors and laypeople, not scholars.

While such a series could take a number of different shapes, we have decided, in most cases, to focus individual volumes on Old Testament figures—people—rather than whole books or themes. Some whole books, of course, will receive major attention in connection with their authors or main characters (e.g., Daniel or Isaiah). Themes will be emphasized in connection with particular figures.

It is our hope and prayer that this series will revive interest in and study of the Old Testament as readers recognize that the Old Testament points forward to Jesus Christ.

A WORD ABOUT THIS VOLUME

Ray Dillard was a beloved teacher, mentor, and colleague to both of the editors of this series. If not for his untimely death on October 1, 1993, he would certainly have been the editor himself. Indeed, his passion and example for grappling with the issues of reading the Old Testament as a Christian inspired us to pursue a series of this kind. It is therefore fitting that the initial volume comes from his own hand. This book exemplifies the kind of strategy we are trying to communicate for reading the Old Testament as Christians.

While Ray had finished a draft of the book in May of 1992, it was never published. We have made some minor additions and consolidations to bring the project to completion. The essence is his. We are grateful to our Savior for using his servant Ray Dillard in our lives and pray that others will profit as we have.

TREMPER LONGMAN III
J. ALAN GROVES

PREFACE

When I began reading the Bible earnestly in my early teenage years, I always struggled with the Old Testament. I was never sure I understood it. I liked the stories. They were full of characters with whom I could identify. I could see bits of myself in their lives: Their temptations and failures were like my own and warned me. Their courage and faithfulness set an example to follow. But I could find similar examples of failure and courage in the morning newspapers or in a good novel. Was this why these stories were there? Were they just to set an example for me?

My real love affair with the Old Testament began a decade later, when some of my teachers at Westminster Theological Seminary taught me how to read the stories of the Bible in better ways. These stories did portray principles of wisdom about life, but the purpose of the Bible was far more to reveal God to us—to show us what he is like and what he has done. When we read the biblical stories, our reading needs to take account of why God revealed himself in the Bible and what he is showing us about himself. The Bible is not me-centered, but God-centered.

But where have I come to know God best? As a Christian, I know God best as I have met him in Jesus, the Messiah. Jesus is "the radiance of God's glory and the exact representation of his being" (Heb. 1:3). It was through him that the world was made, and he was the sum of what the prophets had said (vv. 1–2). For me, there was yet one more step to take: to understand how the God I met in the Old Testament was the same as the God I met in Jesus. I wanted to begin reading the Old Testament in a way that was Christ-centered. We do not meet a new and different God when we cross over that blank page between Malachi and Matthew. Jesus, who was there at the Creation, is "the same yesterday and today and forever" (13:8). Can we read the Old Testament in ways that direct us toward Jesus, in ways that highlight his goodness and grace and his coming again? Can we see how the ways in which God dealt with ancient Israel anticipated his revealing himself to us in Christ?

This desire to read the Old Testament in a Christocentric fashion provided the impetus for this volume on the narratives in 1 and 2 Kings about Elijah and Elisha. I did not want to write a book on hermeneutics (principles of interpretation) or a book on biblical theology (God's revealing of himself through history) or a commentary on these narratives. Rather, I wanted to write a book that would help others to learn, by example, some ways of reading the Old Testament that would directly nourish their faith and growth as Christians.

This book is intended to nourish faith and to provoke worship. It really has three audiences in mind—the individual, the Bible study leader or adult Sunday school teacher, and the pastor. It is divided into eleven chapters; after an introductory chapter, each one contains two or three sections, each section devoted to an event in the life of Elijah or Elisha. (Note that 1 Kings 20; 22; 2 Kings 3; 7:3–20; 8:7–13:9 are not discussed because these passages either do not mention Elijah or Elisha, or mention them only tangentially.) The book can be used in the following ways:

1. *As a guide to devotional reading.* Each chapter is kept fairly short, so that it can be read alongside the passages as part of personal worship.

2. *As a text for a small-group Bible study.* Each chapter ends with a few questions to prompt further reflection and discussion.
3. *As a help toward the preparation of sermons.* The Old Testament is unbelievably rich and exciting—shouldn't we hear more from this three-fourths of the Scriptures during the worship of the church? Trajectories for applications to our current day are interspersed throughout each section.

No book is written in a vacuum. There are a number of folks to whom I want to express my thanks.

For some years, I have been teaching a senior homiletics course at Westminster Seminary. In this course, the students are expected to prepare sermons from Old Testament narratives, and during the years I have taught the course, the Elijah and Elisha stories have been the assigned texts. This has meant that I have myself heard dozens and dozens of sermons on these passages and have had the benefit of talking with students about their sermons for many hours, both as they have developed their thoughts and in interviews after they have preached in class. Every teacher learns far more from his students than they realize. I owe a great debt to the men who have shared with me their encounter with the God of Elijah and Elisha.

After I finished a rough draft of this volume, Mrs. Karen Jobes, then a Ph.D. candidate and instructor in Greek at Westminster, was kind enough to read the chapters and to offer suggestions for the questions and prayers at the end of each chapter. Her suggestions were most helpful to me.

I experience God's goodness, wisdom, and grace most prominently on a daily basis through my wife, Ann, and our three sons, Joel, Jonathan, and Joshua. They are all part of this volume in so many ways beyond the abundant encouragement and patience they show.

The volume is dedicated to three men who have never met one another, but each of whom has been one of God's great gifts to me. How can one measure the value of friends? These men are like brothers to me, and I thank God for them.

I

CHRISTIANS AND THE OLD TESTAMENT

Understanding the relationship between the Old and the New Testaments is perhaps the master key that opens the door to understanding the Bible. Yet Christians often feel disoriented while reading the Old Testament. Somehow it seems less relevant to their lives than the New Testament. After all, we are Christians, and it is the New Testament that speaks to us preeminently and clearly about Jesus Christ, our Savior. The Old Testament seems not only less relevant, but also culturally more distant than the social milieu we encounter in the New Testament. When Christians read the Old Testament, they encounter many genres of literature that are quite different from those of our daily experience. We do not often read law codes, oracles against foreign nations, or rhymeless poetry. In ways that are almost subliminal, the Old Testament seems to communicate to modern Christian readers, "This was not written for you. It was for a different world. This will be hard to read and hard to understand."

And when we do read the Old Testament, most of us feel more at home with its stories. We identify with the characters in their temptations and struggles, and with the interwoven tangle of sin and obedience, success and failure, that filled the days of those whose lives are reported there. But even when we read stories with which we easily identify in terms of our own experience, there is still the nagging doubt, "Is that all there is? Is this what I am supposed to get from reading this passage?"

Sometimes even the stories are disconcerting. Take a few of the Elijah and Elisha narratives as examples. We instinctively feel that it almost trivializes the power of God when that power is used to make an axhead float in water (2 Kings 6:1–7) or to improve the taste of a pot of soup (4:38–41). Doesn't this make God look like a carnival magician? What does it tell us about God when he sends bears to maul children who have insulted a prophet (2:23–25)? And why does God sit idly by when his people are reduced to cannibalism (6:24–7:2)?

The net result is that Christians tend to be ill at ease and unfamiliar with the Old Testament. And that is regrettable. The Old Testament makes up about three-fourths of the Bible, and it is important to Christians for many reasons.

1. The Old Testament is part of the Christian canon. It is God's word—not just for Israel, but also for us. We want to know all we can about God and his purposes for history and our own lives; we cannot neglect the larger part of the Bible and hope to get very far.

2. The Old Testament had enormous influence on the New. The more we study the New Testament, the more we recognize this influence. Jesus' Bible was the Old Testament, and the New Testament was written by Jews who were thoroughly versed in the Hebrew Scriptures. The apostles continually appealed to the Old Testament to verify and bolster their witness to Jesus Christ; they quoted it and alluded to its themes and motifs. Even if our goal were no more than to know the New Testament better, we could not get very far without devoting attention to the Old Testament.

3. The Old Testament reveals Jesus to us. As Christians, we tend to think that we learn most about

our Savior from the New Testament, yet Jesus himself invited us to learn about him from the Old Testament (Luke 24:27, 44). Peter said that all the prophets from Samuel onward spoke of the days and events surrounding the life of Jesus (Acts 3:24). The Old Testament is every bit as much a Christian book as the New Testament.

The God who revealed himself to Israel is the God who was incarnate in Jesus. He is the same, "yesterday and today and forever" (Heb. 13:8). His character and attributes, his mercy, grace, and holiness, are the same for the new Israel, which is the church, as they were for Israel of old. The character and attributes of God did not change between the Testaments.

It is our goal in this small volume to read the Old Testament in ways that appreciate the unity that exists between it and the New Testament. We want to learn from the Elijah and Elisha narratives, but also to see how those accounts direct us onward toward faith in Christ.

REPRESENTATIVE APPROACHES

It is possible, and even necessary, to read these stories from many different vantage points. There are at least three different historical and literary horizons that intersect in the Elijah and Elisha narratives.

1. The historical background of the incidents: when the stories took place.

THE DYNASTIES OF OMRI AND JEHU

Northern Kingdom

I. Omri
    A. Omri, 885–874 B.C.
    B. Ahab, 874–853 B.C.
    C. Ahaziah, 853–852 B.C.
    D. Jehoram, 852–841 B.C.

II. Jehu
   A. Jehu, 841–814 B.C.
   B. Jehoahaz, 814–798 B.C.
   C. Jehoash, 798–782 B.C.
   D. Jeroboam II, 793–753 B.C.
   E. Zechariah, 753–752 B.C.

The Elijah and Elisha stories span a period from the second quarter of the ninth century to the first quarter of the eighth century B.C. These two prophets were active in the northern kingdom during the dynasties of Omri and Jehu.

We first hear of Elijah during the reign of Ahab (1 Kings 17:1); Elisha died during the reign of Jehoash (2 Kings 13:20). Much of the action is set against the backdrop of the reign of Ahab and his notorious wife, Jezebel.

Prior to this period, Israel had always been in danger from the gradual assimilation of Canaanite religious influence into the worship of Yahweh.[1] Canaanite sanctuaries had proliferated in the land before the Israelite conquest, and the religious practices of the Canaanites continually threatened to infiltrate and adulterate the proper worship of God in spite of the strong warnings in the Law and from the Prophets. The northern kingdom was already set on this course from its inception. Shortly after the break-up of the united kingdom under David and Solomon, the first king in the north, Jeroboam, rehabilitated the Canaanite shrines and introduced the worship of Yahweh under the symbol of a bull (1 Kings 12:25–33). The God who called Israel into existence demanded the exclusive allegiance of the nation. His first commandment was that Israel was to have no other gods (Ex. 20:3). Israel was always in danger of losing this antithesis between her God and all the pretenders.

However, during the reign of Omri, there was a noticeable change in royal religious policy in the north. Omri had been seeking a commercial and political alliance with Tyre in order to gain a share of the lucrative trade that moved through that Mediterranean port and to secure an ally against threats from a traditional enemy to the north, the Arameans in Damascus. Such alliances were often sealed in the ancient Near East through a diplomatic marriage, in which a member of one royal household would wed a member of the other (compare 1 Kings 11:1–4). Omri concluded his alliance with Ethbaal of Tyre by arranging the marriage of his son Ahab to the Tyrian princess Jezebel. When Jezebel arrived in Israel, she was not content to worship her own deity in private (1 Kings 16:32). She sought to remove the worship of Yahweh from Israel and to substitute the worship of foreign deities. Jezebel included in her entourage 450 prophets of Baal and 400 prophets of Asherah, the queen mother of the gods (1 Kings 18:19). Under Ahab and his successors in the dynasty, largely due to the tutelage and influence of Jezebel, the religious life of the northern kingdom became a war between the ruling dynasty, which promoted the worship of Baal, and those who adhered to Israel's ancestral faith in Yahweh. Jezebel, in her relationship with Ahab, appears almost to have chosen for herself the role of Anat, the warlike and capricious goddess who was the consort of Baal.

Baal was worshiped under many names throughout the ancient Near East. The Baal that Jezebel introduced was probably Baal Melqart of Tyre. Archaeological discoveries have greatly enhanced our knowledge of Baalism. The mythological texts discovered in the ruins of ancient Ugarit have been especially helpful. Ugarit was a city north of Tyre on the Mediterranean coast that flourished between 1400 and 1200 B.C. In the texts discovered there, Baal was depicted as a nature deity whose primary function and powers in the pantheon encompassed weather and fertility. Baal was the storm deity; he was called the "Rider of the Clouds." He was often portrayed with a lightning bolt in one hand, and thunder was identified as his voice. Ancient Syro-Palestine was an agrarian society, and because Baal gave the rains, he was worshiped to insure the fertility of the land and the production of crops. Since all of life was tied to the fertility of the land, it is not hard to see why it was so tempting to Israel to worship Baal. Describing the impact of Baalism in Israel, Hosea likened Israel to an adulterous wife who said, "I will go after my lovers, who give me my food and my water, my wool and my linen, my oil and my drink" (Hos. 2:5; cf. 2:2–13). Because the fruitfulness of the land was attributed to Baal, he was often associated with motifs of life, healing, and death.

Ugaritic mythology tied the life cycle of Baal to the annual crop cycle: Baal was defeated by the god Mot ("death"), and, as a result, the crops died and the land became unproductive. Then, after a battle in which his consort, Anat, played a prominent role, Baal returned victorious in the autumn, and the fall rains that signaled his return restored fertility to the earth.

Understanding a bit about the Baalism that was sweeping Israel in the ninth century helps to set the Elijah and Elisha stories in sharper focus. Time and again the theological tenets of Baal worship were challenged by these prophets. Yahweh would demonstrate through them that he was the giver of life, rain, and fertility, and that Baal was nothing. We will return to these themes as they are relevant in the chapters that follow.

2. The historical background of the author: when the stories were written. Although the Elijah and Elisha stories are largely set in the ninth century B.C., this was not the period in which the author of the book of Kings (which was later divided into two books, 1 Kings and 2 Kings) lived. The book of Kings is anonymous. We know that the author used many sources in writing his history, and the literary development of the book may be rather complex. The final editor/writer must have lived at a point later than the last events he reports. The book ends by recording the release of Jehoiachin from prison in Babylon during the reign of Amel-Marduk (562–560 B.C.) (2 Kings 25:27). Since the writer does not report the return from captivity to Jerusalem, he probably lived during the later part of the Babylonian exile, sometime between 560 and 540 B.C.

It is valuable for readers today to ask about the Elijah and Elisha stories, not just in terms of the historical significance of the events that they relate, but also in terms of their literary function in the book of Kings. Why did the author choose to include this material in his report? How do these stories fit the overall purpose and interest of the book as a whole? How were they relevant to a writer during the period of the Babylonian exile?

The book of Kings is often called "Deuteronomic history." This is because the writer chose a set of laws unique to Deuteronomy to provide the perspective from which he evaluated Israel's history. Deuteronomy warns Israel about the seductive threat of the foreign religions and foreign gods that the nation would encounter as it entered the land; the book is much concerned that foreign religion not be found among the Israelites (Deut. 12:1–3, 29–32). During Israel's captivity in Babylon (586–539 B.C.), the nation was once again confronted with the seductive tenets of foreign religions and foreign gods. For the writer of Kings, these stories of Israel's encounter with a foreign religion in the past would provide important reminders that in spite of appearances, foreign gods were a delusion.

Have you ever noticed the disproportionate amount of attention given to the Elijah and Elisha stories in Kings? The largest part of 15 out of the 47 chapters in the book (1 Kings 17–2 Kings 9) covers the lives of these two prophets. Almost a third of the history is given to the roughly 80-year period during which they lived, even though the book itself covers over 400 years. Many other prophets are mentioned in Kings, but only here do prophetic stories and miracles cluster with such frequency. The book of Kings, again taking its cue from Deuteronomy (18:9–22), is very much concerned with the power and fulfillment of the words of the prophets. The prophets who followed Moses would also perform signs and wonders (Deut. 34:10–12). Their words would come to pass (Deut. 18:21–22).

Deuteronomy also authorized Israel to have a king (Deut. 17), and the "Deuteronomic history" (Joshua-Kings) traces the history of that institution. The king was charged with maintaining the basic religious orientation of the nation (Deut. 17:18–20), and the well-being of the nation was tied to his faithful obedience to divine law. The entire section of the Elijah and Elisha narratives is introduced by the statement that Ahab exceeded all other kings in his wickedness (1 Kings 16:30–33), and the writer of Kings uses the Elijah and Elisha stories to illustrate this fact. Since the continuation of a dynasty was tied to its fidelity to God (Deut. 17:20), the writer of Kings makes a point of the wickedness of Ahab and his successors and demonstrates how their rule came to an end in the coup d'état staged by Jehu (2 Kings 9–10). The emphasis on Baalism leads naturally to the destruction of Baal's ministers and priests (2 Kings 10:18–31).

The writer of Kings is much concerned to demonstrate that God rules over kings and kingdoms, and that he raises them up and disposes of them as he sees fit. From his vantage point in the sixth century B.C., the writer of Kings is showing how God could also bring judgment and exile on both the northern kingdom (722 B.C.) and the southern kingdom (586 B.C.). In the same way, the God who had raised up the Babylonian armies that destroyed Jerusalem could also bring an end to the Babylonian kingdom.

The Elijah and Elisha stories have a somewhat different atmosphere than most of the rest of Kings, largely because they concentrate so much on the lives of the two prophets, whereas accounts of the prophets are more sporadic and less extended in the remainder of the book. We can only speculate about what sources of information about Elijah and Elisha may have been available to the compiler of the book of Kings. It is at least possible that a proponent of the reforms undertaken by Jehu pulled together the stories about Elijah and Elisha into a single narrative in order to show how bad conditions had become during the Omride dynasty and to explain and justify Jehu's coup and the attendant destruction of Baal worship (2 Kings 10:16–31).

3. Later biblical interpretation: for example, Matthew. The first person to read a text after it has been written begins the process of its interpretation. Subsequent biblical authors were quite familiar with the Elijah and Elisha stories, and they also used these accounts to instruct later generations. They drew a variety of inferences from them and found illustrations there that they could apply to the needs of their own audiences.

It is striking that the Old Testament itself ends by recalling Elijah and proclaiming that he would come again (Mal. 4:5–6). The gospel writers also made frequent reference to our two prophets. We shall have occasion to reflect on most of this material in the brief meditations that follow in this volume. However, before moving on to the individual narratives, we will pause to see how Matthew in particular made use of the Elijah and Elisha stories. Since Matthew was writing about the life of Jesus and made frequent use of these accounts from Kings, his example may provide a framework for Christians who want to relate the Old Testament to the New and to their own lives.

Matthew draws parallels between the lives of Elijah and Elisha and the lives of John the Baptist and Jesus. He presents John as the fulfillment of Malachi's prophecy that Elijah would come again (Mal. 4:5), and he presents Jesus as the new Elisha.² The Jews of Jesus' day apparently expected that Elijah would appear literally and physically from the grave, and so when John the Baptist was asked if he was Elijah, he replied, "I am not" (John 1:21). At least early in his ministry, John the Baptist does not appear to have been aware that he was fulfilling the role of the expected Elijah. On the other hand, Jesus described John as "the Elijah who was to come" (Matt. 11:14; cf. 17:12), and Matthew goes out of his way to demonstrate how this was so:

a. Elijah was known for his distinctive style of dress. When Ahaziah sent messengers to inquire of Baal-Zebub, the god of Ekron, his messengers encountered a mysterious figure who sent them back to the king. When the king asked the messengers, "What kind of man was it who came to meet you?" the messengers answered, "He was a man with a garment of hair and with a leather belt around his waist" (2 Kings 1:7–8). The king knew immediately from this rather minimal description that his messengers had encountered Elijah. Matthew introduces John the Baptist at the beginning of his preaching by saying, "John's clothes were made of camel's hair, and he had a leather belt around his waist" (Matt. 3:4). This unusual clothing was reminiscent of Elijah.

b. Both Elijah and John the Baptist faced a hostile political power throughout their lives. In particular, the main antagonist for both was a woman at the royal court who was seeking their lives. For Elijah, it was Jezebel (1 Kings 19:2, 10, 14); for John, it was Herodias (Matt. 14:3–12).

c. Both Elijah and John the Baptist anointed their successors at the Jordan River. (1) On both occasions, the heavens were opened and the participants saw a flying object descending from above. Elijah and Elisha saw an approaching chariot (2 Kings 2:11–12); John and Jesus saw a descending dove (Matt. 3:16). (2) In the Old Testament, the Spirit of God is often the Spirit of prophecy; possession by the Spirit enabled one to fulfill his calling. While 50 other prophets waited nearby, Elisha asked for a "double portion" of the Spirit that was on Elijah (2 Kings 2:9). The double portion was the inheritance assigned to the firstborn son; Elisha's request would set him apart from the rest of the prophets. When John saw the Spirit descending as a dove on Jesus, he heard the words, "This is my Son" (Matt. 3:17), God's own firstborn, one set apart from the rest. Elijah was the forerunner of Elisha, just as John the Baptist was for Jesus. Luke notes this theme as well: when the birth of John the Baptist was foretold to his father Zechariah, the angel Gabriel said that John would "go on before the Lord, in the spirit and power of Elijah," and that John would fulfill the mission assigned to Elijah by Malachi, "to turn the hearts of the fathers to their children" (Luke 1:17; cf. Mal. 4:6).

d. The test of whether Elisha would succeed Elijah was "if you see me when I am taken from you, it will be yours—otherwise not" (2 Kings 2:10). The question was whether or not Elisha would also be admitted to the heavenly council and enabled to peer into the glory cloud (cf. Jer. 23:18–19). Jesus, like Elisha, saw Elijah in heavenly glory on the Mount of Transfiguration (Matt. 17:2–3).

e. There is perhaps no section of the Old Testament that abounds in miracles as much as the Elisha narrative. Having given Elisha the double portion of the Spirit that he sought, God demonstrates his empowerment of the prophet and testifies to the message he proclaimed through the miracles that accompanied Elisha's ministry. Similarly, miracles abound when God himself testifies to the ministry of his own Son (Heb. 2:3–4).

The appearance of Elijah was supposed to inaugurate "that great and dreadful day of the Lord" (Mal. 4:5), the day when God would judge evil while protecting and preserving his people. While John was in prison, he heard that Jesus was preaching and teaching in Galilee. So John sent messengers to ask Jesus, "Are you the one who was to come, or should we expect someone else?" Jesus told John's disciples to "go back and report to John what you hear and see: The blind receive sight, the lame walk, those who have leprosy are cured, the deaf hear, the dead are raised, and the good news is preached to the poor" (Matt. 11:2–5). This list is largely a list of the miracles of Elisha, who had restored sight to the blind (2 Kings 6:18–20), cured leprosy (chap. 5), restored the dead to life (4:32–37; 8:4–5; 13:21), and brought good news to the destitute (4:1–7; 7:1–2; 8:6). This list conflates the miracles of Elisha with those of the promised Servant of the Lord (Isa. 61:1–3). Jesus was in effect telling John, "Elijah's successor has come. I am the one you are looking for." John was the herald that Isaiah had said would prepare the way for the coming of the servant of the Lord (Isa. 40:3; Matt. 3:3); John was Elijah, the forerunner of an even greater prophet.

Matthew drew these parallels between Elijah and John, and between Elisha and Jesus. In doing this, Matthew provided one of a number of interpretive grids with which Christians can read this portion of the Old Testament. Other gospel writers used the narrative of Elijah and Elisha in equally creative and helpful ways, which we will comment upon as we review the individual stories. For example, Kings itself presents a number of parallels between Elijah and Moses; these are described in the chapter discussing 1 Kings 19:1–18. Later biblical authors also paired Elijah and Moses in reference to the day of the Lord (Mal. 4:4–5), on the Mount of Transfiguration (Matt. 17:3–4; Mark 9:4–5; Luke 9:30–33), and in Revelation (Rev. 11:3–6). Moses represented the Law, and Elijah represented the Prophets; in the person of Jesus, one came who was greater than Moses and Elijah, and all the Law and the Prophets spoke of him (Luke 24:27).

2

THE LORD,
OUR PROVIDER

The story of Elijah and Elisha begins with three narratives that are united by the theme of death, whether impending or actual. The first two accounts center on problems with water and food. Without them, we die, yet often, especially in affluent societies like our own, we take them for granted.

In Elijah's day, the Israelites, under the influence of the royal family, were swayed to the pagan view that Baal, the Canaanite god of weather and fertility, was the source of water and food. Unless Baal was worshiped, rain would not fall. Without rain, there would be no crops. And without crops, there would be no life. But God prepared two lessons to teach Israel that he controlled the weather and fertility.

The third episode flows from the second. The second story introduces the widow of Zarephath, whose household God used to provide Elijah with food during a famine. In the third story of the cycle, the woman's child dies, creating yet another situation in which the prophet can demonstrate God's sovereignty over life and death.

All three of these episodes illustrate that God, not Baal, provides life for his people.

A. OF PEDIGREES AND PROVISIONS
1 KINGS 17:1–6

> Now Elijah the Tishbite, from Tishbe in Gilead, said to Ahab, "As the LORD, the God of Israel, lives, whom I serve, there will be neither dew nor rain in the next few years except at my word."
>
> Then the word of the LORD came to Elijah: "Leave here, turn eastward and hide in the Kerith Ravine, east of the Jordan. You will drink from the brook, and I have ordered the ravens to feed you there."
>
> So he did what the LORD had told him. He went to the Kerith Ravine, east of the Jordan, and stayed there. The ravens brought him bread and meat in the morning and bread and meat in the evening, and he drank from the brook.

Elijah appears on the scene with surprising abruptness. He is introduced without any information about his prior life, without reference to his family or clan in Israel, and even his place of birth (Tishbe) is not known with confidence today. He is assigned no elaborate pedigree, whereby we could place him in the social register of ancient Israel, and no support group is mentioned for whom he could be considered the spokesman. He lived in Gilead, a peripheral area in ancient Israel, isolated across the Jordan. He had no fame or notoriety, no particular political clout, no credentials to command a hearing, no alphabet soup of academic degrees following his name. His seemingly humble beginnings remind us of another servant of the Lord, one who had "no beauty or majesty to attract us to him, nothing in his appearance that we should desire him," a man who was "despised and rejected" (Isa. 53:2–3), a man whose pedigree was also questioned (John 6:42; 8:39–41). Like the nation of Israel itself, God chose as his servants "not many . . . [who] were wise by human standards, not many . . . [who] were influential, not many [who] were of noble birth. But God chose the foolish things of the world to shame the wise; God chose the weak things of the world to shame the strong. He chose the lowly things of this world and the despised things—and the things that are not—to nullify the things that are" (1 Cor. 1:26–28).

Elijah's great qualification for serving God at his moment in history was the same as that other servant of the Lord: his food and drink were "to do the will of him who sent me" (John 4:34). All too often as Christians, we tend to think that the work of God in our day is done by the great and powerful, the famous preachers, celebrities, and the influential wealthy. God looks not for fame but for faith, not wealth but willingness, not renown but reliance. The only pedigree needed to serve God in our world is his call to obedience. It is to believe that "the LORD, the God of Israel, lives" (1 Kings 17:1), and to serve him instead of the Baals.

God had long ago set before Israel the ways of life and death, of blessing and cursing, of obedience and disobedience. Near the time of his death, Moses reminded Israel that God's laws were "not just idle words for you—they are your life" (Deut. 32:47). Prosperity—the full barns, bounteous crops, livestock, and ample food that the people desired—was tied to following his commands (28:1–6), but disobedience would bring hunger to the nation, the failure of both crops and rain. "The sky over your head will be bronze, the ground beneath you iron. The LORD will turn the rain of your country into dust and powder" (28:23–24).

God could not be God if he was not true to his own word. With the wickedness of Ahab exceeding that of all the kings who had preceded him (1 Kings 16:30–33), God responded according to his sworn promise and sent Elijah to announce a drought.

In ancient Israel, the primary agricultural season was during the winter months. After the heat and dry season during the summer, the early rains came in the autumn to soften the parched and cracked ground. If these rains did not come, the ground was indeed like iron and could not be plowed. Springs and wells would not be refreshed. The latter rains fell in the spring, and these gave the crops the moisture needed to develop and flourish. If these rains did not come, the harvest was destroyed.

Much of the Elijah narrative is set in the region around the plain of Jezreel. Each morning from fall to spring in this valley, the coating of dew is so heavy that even if it did not rain, agriculture would still be possible. This is the area where Gideon had laid his fleece, alternately requesting that it be wet and dry (Judg. 6:36–40). This helps us to understand why Elijah announced that God would withhold not only the rain, but also the dew.

There could be no clearer way to throw down the gauntlet to the worship of Baal. In Canaanite mythology, Baal was the God of the storm. In one of the ancient texts from Ugarit, Baal's power over the waters is described:

> Seven years shall Baal fail, eight the Rider of the
> Clouds.
> There shall be no dew, no rain,
>   no surging of the two depths,
>   nor the goodness of Baal's voice.[1]

In the annual crop cycle, when Baal died and vegetation ceased to grow, the god Mot told Baal to descend into the netherworld and to "take your clouds, your wind, your storm, your rains."[2] In another text, a king of Ugarit named Keret has a vision and reports,

The heavens rain oil,
   the wadies run with honey,
So I know that the mighty one, Baal, lives,
   Lo, the Prince, the Lord of the Earth, exists.[3]

The third line of this Ugaritic poem is very similar to the Hebrew with which Elijah introduces the drought: "As the LORD, the God of Israel, lives." The great contest between Yahweh and Baal is now set, and we will soon discover which God lives. Ahab, Jezebel, and their minions were serving Baal to insure the fertility of the land. Elijah would serve Yahweh, the God of Israel. In announcing God's power over the rains, the challenge was unmistakable.

The three episodes in 1 Kings 17 all show some of the effects of the drought, and each addresses human needs that were the particular province of Baal's power in Canaanite mythology. While the nation began to feel the effects of the drought, Elijah experienced the blessings of food and water that God had promised to an obedient nation. God had promised,

> If you follow my decrees and are careful to obey my commands, I will send you rain in its season, and the ground will yield its crops and the trees of the field their fruit. Your threshing will continue until grape harvest and the grape harvest will continue until planting, and you will eat all the food you want and live in safety in your land. (Lev. 26:3–5)

But,

> If after all this you will not listen to me, I will punish you for your sins seven times over. I will

break down your stubborn pride and make the sky above you like iron and the ground beneath you like bronze. Your strength will be spent in vain, because your soil will not yield its crops, nor will the trees of the land yield their fruit. (Lev. 26:18–20)

Yahweh, the God of Israel, sent rain to fall on the just and the unjust (Matt. 5:45); he could also withhold it.

Elijah now embodied what Israel was supposed to be, devoted to Yahweh and serving him alone. So God does not abandon his prophet, but provides for him those tokens of divine blessing that would have gone to an obedient nation. Just as God had provided Israel under Moses with food and drink in the wilderness (Ex. 17; Num. 11; 20), so he now provides for his faithful servant.

The Lord, who knows the fall of a single sparrow, also commands the ravens. When Israel was wandering in the wilderness, God was "like an eagle that stirs up its nest and hovers over its young, that spreads its wings to catch them and carries them on its pinions" (Deut. 32:11). Now the birds do the bidding of their Creator, for he has taken Elijah under his wings.

For us, too, in a dry and thirsty world, he has spread a table of food and drink (Matt. 26; 1 Cor. 11), with instructions that we also must flee from idolatry (1 Cor. 10:14–17). God's grace was new for the prophet each morning (Lam. 3:22–24). Although the brook Cherith would eventually diminish and run dry, Jesus has opened for us a well that will never run dry (John 4:10, 13–14; 7:37–39).

Jesus, too, would embody what Israel was supposed to be—a nation/man living in obedience to God's command. But, unlike Elijah, he would not be spared in his identification with his people; rather, he would experience divine judgment, and Elijah would not come to save him (Matt. 27:47–49).

While Elijah was at the brook, the crops of Israel would fail, and the watercourses and wells of the land would run dry. Many would begin to suffer from the privation to follow, as subsequent episodes show. Yet even in this, the love of God is evident. Just as a father chastens the children he loves (Heb. 12:5–11), so God chastens Israel. How much better it is to know the rebuke and chastening of God than to be abandoned by him! Chastening is the price of our election.

Elijah's sudden appearance revealed God—but so did his disappearance. We do not know the location of the brook Cherith, or how long the prophet was there. It was at least long enough for the effects of the drought to become widespread and severe (1 Kings 17:7–12). God had commanded the prophet to hide (17:3; contrast 18:1). Now Israel would endure not simply a famine of food and water, but a famine of the word of God (Amos 8:11; Ps. 74:9).

FOR FURTHER REFLECTION

1. Water plays a significant role throughout the Elijah narrative. What is it about water that makes it so important to the story? What is its connection to Baal? To Yahweh?
2. Baal is no longer the overt opponent of the Lord God in our society. But what has taken his place? In your own life, what things oppose God's lordship? How does God show his power over these things today?
3. God wonderfully provided for Elijah's need during the drought. In what circumstances in your life, in your family, or in your church have you been aware of God's care?

4. Even though Elijah was faithful and obedient, he did not entirely escape the plight of his fellow Israelites. Have you ever suffered because of the sins of others? How do you react in such a situation?

5. Jesus is the true bread and living water for his disciples. Does this passage about Elijah point to Jesus in this way? What does this mean to you?

B. OF FAMINE AND FAITH
1 KINGS 17:7–16

Some time later the brook dried up because there had been no rain in the land. Then the word of the LORD came to him: "Go at once to Zarephath of Sidon and stay there. I have commanded a widow in that place to supply you with food." So he went to Zarephath. When he came to the town gate, a widow was there gathering sticks. He called to her and asked, "Would you bring me a little water in a jar so I may have a drink?" As she was going to get it, he called, "And bring me, please, a piece of bread."

"As surely as the LORD your God lives," she replied, "I don't have any bread—only a handful of flour in a jar and a little oil in a jug. I am gathering a few sticks to take home and make a meal for myself and my son, that we may eat it—and die."

Elijah said to her, "Don't be afraid. Go home and do as you have said. But first make a small cake of bread for me from what you have and bring it to me, and then make something for yourself and your son. For this is what the LORD, the God of Israel, says: 'The jar of flour will not be used up and the jug of oil will not run dry until the day the LORD gives rain on the land.'"

She went away and did as Elijah had told her. So there was food every day for Elijah and for the woman and her family. For the jar of flour was not used up and the jug of oil did not run dry, in keeping with the word of the LORD spoken by Elijah.

God could have maintained Elijah's brook indefinitely, but he wanted the prophet to move (1 Kings 17:9). But why to Zarephath?

Zarephath was located on the Mediterranean coast between Tyre and Sidon, the great cities of the Phoenicians. In sending Elijah there, God was teaching his people that his power was not confined to the borders of Israel—that he was not just a god of the hills or plains (1 Kings 20:23), restricted to his home turf. The crisis that had arisen in Israel had been caused by the worship of the Phoenician god Baal (16:31–32). This Baal was worshiped as the god who provided rain and fertility. But when Israel's God announced a drought and famine (17:1), its effects would be felt far beyond the land of Israel, for his power was not confined to the land he had promised to Abraham and his descendants. By demonstrating his power in Phoenicia and his power to remedy the effects of the drought as he pleased, Israel's God was also showing the impotence of Baal in his own homeland. This was a way of saying that the gods of the nations are an illusion—that they have no power and are not gods at all. Yahweh, the God of Israel, ruled also in the homeland of Jezebel's father. Her god had no power there, and he could scarcely be commended as a worthy object of Israel's worship.

Remember that the book of Kings was written to exiles during the Babylonian captivity. When the writer reports this story to his audience of exiles in the sixth century B.C., the message is the same: the gods of the nations are idols and have no power, while Yahweh rules over all the earth. So much, too, for the gods of our own age.

Phoenicia was a great maritime power, but was unable to feed herself. A number of biblical texts reveal how the Phoenicians were often dependent on Israel as a source of imported foodstuffs (2 Chron. 2:10; Ezek. 27:17; cf. Acts 12:20). Isn't it ironic that Israel would be tempted to worship the Phoenician Baal as a source of fertility, when Phoenicia could not provide her own food? But then, aren't idols always a delusion? When we as individuals make wealth, education, position, fame, or any number of other things the objects of our adoration and effort, can they satisfy the longing of our souls? Are they ever adequate to the task?

Israel's God was never meant to be the exclusive possession of Israel. From the moment that God chose Abraham and promised to bless his descendants, his blessing was not for Israel alone, but for a much wider group of people. Abraham and his descendants would bring divine blessing to "all peoples on earth" (Gen. 12:3; 18:18; 22:18). Israel was to be a witness to the nations. The idea of missions in the Old Testament is that the nations would be drawn to Israel's God through observing his people. Israel was to be a light in a dark world. But when Baal worship became the state religion of the northern kingdom and stole the hearts of the nation, Israel could not fulfill this mission, for she was then little different from the nations around her.

Although Israel was failing to carry out her commission from God, his promise to the Gentiles would not be frustrated. God sent his prophet to a widow from Tyre, and he showed through the person of Elijah how his grace would be spread to the nations.

It has always been the command of God to love our enemies. That is part of God's own character that we see in his love directed toward us. But that was not a popular message in ancient Israel. Elisha would also struggle with the same problem when God blessed an enemy general with healing from leprosy (2 Kings 5).

When Jesus traveled through the region of "Galilee of the Gentiles" (Matt. 4:15) and brought the good news of God's grace to the nations, it was not well received by the residents of his hometown, Nazareth. They demanded the same miracles for themselves as he had performed elsewhere. Jesus replied by alluding to the experience of Elijah, that "no prophet is accepted in his hometown" (Luke 4:24). He reminded them that there had been many widows in Israel during the days of Elijah, when the sky was shut up for three and a half years, but Elijah was sent not to them, but to a gentile widow. Their response was almost predictable. For generations, Israel had killed her prophets. The spirit of Jezebel (1 Kings 18:4; 19:2, 10) was alive in Israel when Jesus' own townsmen sought to take his life (Luke 4:28–30). Jesus was about to break down that wall that separated Jew from Gentile.

God wanted the kind of faith that the widow showed to characterize Israel. But he found it instead in a gentile woman. Similarly, Jesus once met a centurion whose servant was on the verge of death; he would say of this Gentile's trust in his word, "I have not found such great faith even in Israel" (Luke 7:9).

When you read about the widow's oil and flour, keep in mind the nature of miracles in the Bible. Miracles are God's way of testifying to the truth of his word; miracles accredit God's messengers (Heb. 1:1; 2:4). They are not willy-nilly magical displays, arbitrarily invoked to titillate the curious.

Miracles are also redemptive. They redeem and restore; they overcome the results of sin in our world and anticipate the re-creation of a universe that will be free from sin and its effects. As redemptive events, they point toward and anticipate the renewal of the heavens and the earth at the end of time. Is it any surprise, then, that Israel's prophets often depicted future blessing in terms of agricultural bounty (e. g., Amos 9:13–15; Joel 3:18; Ezek. 47:12; Zech. 3:10)? There was no want or lack in the garden that God provided for Adam and Eve, and in the New Jerusalem there will be no more death, mourning, crying, or pain (Rev. 21:4–5; 22:1–5). The widow of Zarephath and her son received only a foretaste of what is yet to be.

God shows his mercy to a widow and her son. Once again, God has chosen those who are weak and lowly in the eyes of this world as the objects of his favor. Those who are rich and powerful too easily think they can manage in life without God. Those who are without in this world—without rights, without resources, without providers, without parents—are the ones who see their need to depend on God and who have foregone the pride that others retain. The poor were the particular object of Jesus' ministry. God instructs us to be kind to the poor and needy, because he cares about them (Isa. 10:1–4; Prov. 14:31). God's servant would come to proclaim good news to the poor (Isa. 61:1; Luke 4:18).

Imagine the widow's perspective. How would you have responded when the prophet showed up and asked for food while you were preparing what would apparently be the final meal for you and your son? "Just what I need, another mouth to feed," or perhaps, "Be warm, be fed— but above all, be gone!" It has never been any different: true, living faith is shown in deeds (James 2:17–18), not just in words.

It must have been hard for Elijah to say "Feed me first" in the face of such dire need (1 Kings 17:13). But this demand was backed by a promise from the Lord, the God of Israel: he was saying, in effect, "Put me first and see my power. Believe my word and it will be the power that will bring you salvation and deliverance." Was there any reason for this widow to believe this poor, mendicant foreigner? Yet when she believed the promise of God, it brought food for her and her family during the years of drought.

God's promises often look a bit foolish, even downright unbelievable. And they always require faith. The good news of God's promises, the gospel, when believed and obeyed, becomes the very power of God (1 Cor. 1:18). Elijah did not come with eloquence and persuasiveness, but "with a demonstration of the Spirit's power, so that your faith might not rest on men's wisdom, but on God's power" (1 Cor. 2:4–5).

FOR FURTHER REFLECTION

1. Elijah must have wondered what God was doing when the brook dried up. So often in life, after times of disappointment or discouragement have passed, we can see the providential hand of God in those very circumstances. Have you thanked God for the tough times, the times that stretch and build faith? Now would be a good time to do so.

2. Israel was deluded in looking to Baal for help and sustenance. In what idol have you placed your trust, only to find out later that it was undeserving of your devotion?

3. God was showing his lordship outside the boundaries of Israel when he sent Elijah to Zarephath. How do we see that lordship expressed among all nations today?

4. The widow showed her faith in God's word by feeding Elijah before she cared for her son and herself. Have there been times when you felt that

obeying God's word was foolhardy? Did you obey? What happened? If you chose not to obey, have you asked for forgiveness?

5. The spirit of Jezebel—the desire to resist the word of God by persecuting the messenger—is alive and well in our own day. Where have you experienced it—or been a party to it?

C. NOW I KNOW
1 KINGS 17:17–24

Some time later the son of the woman who owned the house became ill. He grew worse and worse, and finally stopped breathing. She said to Elijah, "What do you have against me, man of God? Did you come to remind me of my sin and kill my son?"

"Give me your son," Elijah replied. He took him from her arms, carried him to the upper room where he was staying, and laid him on his bed. Then he cried out to the LORD, "O LORD my God, have you brought tragedy also upon this widow I am staying with, by causing her son to die?" Then he stretched himself out on the boy three times and cried to the LORD, "O LORD my God, let this boy's life return to him!"

The LORD heard Elijah's cry, and the boy's life returned to him, and he lived. Elijah picked up the child and carried him down from the room into the house. He gave him to his mother and said, "Look, your son is alive!"

Then the woman said to Elijah, "Now I know that you are a man of God and that the word of the LORD from your mouth is the truth."

Some of the most beautiful weather that people can enjoy ordinarily occurs during the hours just before a hurricane hits the shore. The cyclonic rotation and low pressure of the giant storm clears the skies around it.

For the widow, this period of knowing and experiencing God's grace through the never-empty jars of oil and flour was the calm before the storm. Her faith, we know, was already great—but it would be tested severely again. For a time, peace was enjoyed where death had been expected (1 Kings 17:7–16). How quickly peace was destroyed when death came again!

It is often this way when our faith is about to be tested. Abraham had received God's promise in his son Isaac, but that child's life was under threat (Gen. 22). Job had been righteous, but all he had in family and possessions were gone, and even his own flesh was decaying on his body. After the triumph at Mount Carmel (1 Kings 18), Elijah would again be fleeing for his life (1 Kings 19). How easy it is to turn from the path of faith! It is so tempting to discount the faithfulness and power of God. Exercising faith is not something we do once. It is a way of life, a walk by faith instead of sight (2 Cor. 5:7). It is being sure of what we hope for and certain of what we do not see (Heb. 11:1). It is by faith that "women received back their dead, raised to life again" (Heb. 11:35).

In the mythology of ancient Canaan, Baal was not only the god of the storm and rain. Because all of life depended on the rains, Baal was also the giver and sustainer of life. When he gave the rain, the earth yielded its bounty, and people thrived, along with all other creatures; when he withheld the rain, people, plants, and animals suffered and died. Drought, dehydration, desiccation, and disease crowded life from the earth.

The Canaanites, in their mythology, often portrayed warfare among the gods. At the end of the growing season each year, the god Mot ("death") defeated Baal, and Baal descended into the netherworld, where he stayed throughout the dry season. But in the fall, Baal, with the help of his consort, Anat, was victorious and returned from the realm of the dead to bring the life-giving showers for the growing season. Baal was the source of life, and he was annually triumphant over the grave.

Israel should have known better. God had long before told Noah that he was the power behind the changing seasons: "As long as the earth endures, seedtime and harvest, cold and heat, summer and winter, day and night will never cease" (Gen. 8:22). But Israel's God did not have to die each year for these things to happen—they were the routine operations of the providence by which he ruled over his creation.

Once again the issue of power was raised on Baal's home turf—at Zarephath, a town between the leading cities of the very Phoenicians who had exported Jezebel and her god to Israel. Baal's power over life was at best indirect. In the weather patterns of ancient Canaan, the rains either came or did not come, and people felt the impact in the more gradual cycles of plenty and want. But what about the death of people—the silent hearts, the stopped breathing (1 Kings 17:17)? Even in Canaanite mythology, Baal himself could not escape from the netherworld without help. What could he do for the widow's son? In reality, Baal was just as dead as the trees that had been cut down to make his images. He was simply the product of human imagination.

Human beings seem ever ready and willing to trust in idols. Today we may not stand in front of statues made by human hands, but we have plenty of other idols. Idols are those things we serve in order to establish and maintain our own sense of wholeness and well-being. Idols in our lives are often money and material things, jobs, power, position, influence, and even other people. But these all end at the grave. Like Baal, they cannot transcend that great leveler of all people. What in this life do you have that will go with you through the grave?

Jesus, too, would take the battle to the enemy's home turf. Satan's great power is death (Heb. 2:14), and his domain is the grave. When Jesus descended into the grave and was there for three days awaiting his resurrection, he showed himself to be the Lord over death as well as over life. He broke the power of Satan. Jesus has dominion over the grave.

The God of Israel had introduced both life and death into the world (Gen. 3:3), and neither was beyond his control. So the prophet Elijah took the dead child to an upper room to cry out to God on his behalf. Is it not ironic that it was in another upper room, while Jesus was preparing the disciples for his own imminent death, that he taught them, "I am the way and the truth and the life" (John 14:6)? Jesus called his friend Lazarus from the grave, and he taught those who saw it, "I am the resurrection and the life. He who believes in me will live, even though he dies; and whoever lives and believes in me will never die" (John 11:25). Although Elijah almost certainly did not have any clear idea of the doctrine of the Trinity, Christians in all ages have seen in his stretching out in prayer three times over the child (1 Kings 17:21) a reminder of prayer in the name of the Father, the Son, and the Holy Spirit. The Son of God was also stretched out, stretched out on a cross imparting life to the world (cf. 2 Kings 4:8–37). Once again, miracles are anticipatory and redemptive: the widow and her son had a foretaste of the destruction of that last and greatest enemy, death (1 Cor. 15:26). In Canaanite mythology, Baal could defeat death for a time, only to succumb to it again. How unlike the gospel—for Christ has destroyed death.

Is it not also ironic that the widow thought of her son's death as a reminder of her sin (1 Kings 17:18)? But the widow's son was not given as the price for her sin. Only God could give a Son to pay that price.

As Jesus reminds us, there were many hungry widows in Israel when Elijah was sent to the home of this gentile woman (Luke 4:25). And no doubt many among them also lost a child—children are among the first to succumb to the diseases that rage in the face of starvation and hunger. But God's grace was not for Israel alone, but for Jew and Gentile alike. Jesus once traveled in the vicinity of Tyre (Mark 7:24–30). There a Greek woman, born in Syrian Phoenicia, came to Jesus with her daughter, who was possessed by an evil spirit. God's grace came to Gentiles once again.

It is one thing to have our daily needs met. We all must pray and work for our daily bread. I suppose that when the widow saw that her jars of oil and flour were never empty, she could have said, "I know that you are a man of God, and that the word of the LORD from your mouth is the truth." But this exclamation comes only at the end of the story (1 Kings 17:24). Similarly, our daily needs are often met, perhaps even taken for granted, through the ordinary means of God's providence. Even when our situations may become grave, sudden relief can be attributed to some idol, a product of our own effort, like Baal. But when life comes from the grave, we know that we are in the presence of God. He and he alone can do this.

After he fed the five thousand, Jesus taught them that he was the bread of life. Many found it a hard teaching (John 6:60); even his followers grumbled. Aware of their grumbling, Jesus said, "The words I have spoken to you are spirit and they are life" (v. 33). For many, this required more faith than they could muster—they were not ready to trust Jesus, and so they turned away (v. 66). When Jesus asked the Twelve whether they also wanted to leave, Peter answered with words quite similar to the widow's: "Lord, to whom shall we go? You have the words of eternal life" (v. 68).

FOR FURTHER REFLECTION

1. How have tragedy and disaster stretched your faith and deepened your walk with God?
2. Do you remember a time or times in your life when you felt that God was punishing you through some tragedy? Rethink that experience in the light of Romans 8:1, "There is now no condemnation for those who are in Christ Jesus."
3. What is your attitude toward death? Are you afraid to think about it? Why?
4. Where do you turn when the thought of your death overwhelms you?
5. What does it mean to you that Christ has tasted death for us and has destroyed its power?

3

YAHWEH VERSUS BAAL: THE ULTIMATE CONTEST

irst Kings 18 is arguably the most dramatic episode in the narrative of Elijah and Elisha. Indeed, it is one of the most exciting stories in the entire Old Testament. Here the prophet Elijah confronts King Ahab, behind whom stands Queen Jezebel. Even on the human level, the tension is palpable.

But there is more than a human level here. At its most fundamental point, this chapter is about the conflict between the true God of the universe and the false idols that human beings too often construct to escape the demands of the One who made us. This is the story of Yahweh's defeat of Baal, an impotent god revealed for what he really is—a god that does not exist.

This chapter is divided into two sections: "Confrontation and Concealment" (1 Kings 18:1–15) and "Idolatry on Trial" (1 Kings 18:16–46).

A. CONFRONTATION AND CONCEALMENT
1 KINGS 18:1–15

After a long time, in the third year, the word of the LORD came to Elijah: "Go and present yourself to Ahab, and I will send rain on the land." So Elijah went to present himself to Ahab.

Now the famine was severe in Samaria, and Ahab had summoned Obadiah, who was in charge of his palace. (Obadiah was a devout believer in the LORD. While Jezebel was killing off the LORD's prophets, Obadiah had taken a hundred prophets and hidden them in two caves, fifty in each, and had supplied them with food and water.) Ahab had said to Obadiah, "Go through the land to all the springs and valleys. Maybe we can find some grass to keep the horses and mules alive so we will not have to kill any of our animals." So they divided the land they were to cover, Ahab going in one direction and Obadiah in another.

As Obadiah was walking along, Elijah met him. Obadiah recognized him, bowed down to the ground, and said, "Is it really you, my lord Elijah?"

"Yes," he replied. "Go tell your master, 'Elijah is here.'"

"What have I done wrong," asked Obadiah, "that you are handing your servant over to Ahab to be put to death? As surely as the LORD your God lives, there is not a nation or kingdom where my master has not sent someone to look for you. And whenever a nation or kingdom claimed you were not there, he made them swear they could not find you. But now you tell me to go to my master and say, 'Elijah is here.' I don't know where the Spirit of the LORD may carry you when I leave you. If I go and tell Ahab and he doesn't find you, he will kill me. Yet I your servant have worshiped the LORD since my youth. Haven't you heard, my lord, what I did while Jezebel was killing the prophets of the LORD? I hid a hundred of the LORD's prophets in two caves, fifty in each, and supplied them with food and water. And now you tell me to go to my master and say, 'Elijah is here.' He will kill me!"

Elijah said, "As the LORD Almighty lives, whom I serve, I will surely present myself to Ahab today."

Contrast God's command to the prophet to "hide" (1 Kings 17:2) with his command to "present yourself to Ahab" (18:1). The prophet has returned to public life in Israel, and the famine of hearing the word of God ends with his reappearance. The famine from the drought will soon end as well, for "I will send rain on the land" (18:1).

Before the writer of Kings reports the confrontation of Elijah with Ahab and the prophets of Baal and Asherah, he includes one other story in order to show how bad the famine had become and to further characterize the protagonists. He introduces Ahab and Obadiah in order to forge a powerful contrast between the two. In Israel, along with much of the rest of the ancient Near East, kingship was commonly portrayed with shepherd imagery. A good king was a shepherd to his people, protecting and caring for them, providing for their needs, and seeking their well-being.

When the famine became severe (1 Kings 18:2), Ahab was out looking for water and forage for his own horses and mules (v. 5). His people were starving, but God forbid that he should suffer the loss of any of his animals! Ahab was a shepherd all right—literally shepherding his livestock instead of his people. This shepherd would not give his life for the sheep.

But contrast him with Obadiah. With food and water scarce and commodity prices probably out of sight, this man still managed to feed and maintain a hundred prophets, concealing them from the murderous rage of the king and queen. Ahab had been scouring the earth not only to feed his livestock, but also to find Elijah (v.

10). Contrast the way in which the two men greeted the prophet: Ahab greeted him as "you troubler of Israel" (v. 17), but Obadiah addressed him as "my lord Elijah" (v. 7). Ahab was seeking the welfare of his own kingdom, but Obadiah had learned, centuries before Jesus commanded it, to "seek first his kingdom and his righteousness, and all these things will be given to you as well" (Matt. 6:33).

Ahab was worried about grass when he should have been worried about the wrath of God. It is not hard to understand how this could be so. Just look around. Every day millions of people set out in pursuit of their personal goals and the almighty dollar, ignoring or denying that the wrath of an almighty God is the vital issue. People prefer to worry about making a living rather than meeting God. But Obadiah had already learned, "Do not be afraid of those who kill the body but cannot kill the soul. Rather, be afraid of the One who can destroy both soul and body in hell" (Matt. 10:28). Obadiah would not disown the God he loved (Matt. 10:32–33). It is true to this day: "No one can serve two masters. Either he will hate the one and love the other, or he will be devoted to the one and despise the other. You cannot serve both God and Money" (Matt. 6:24).

The history of God's prophets is largely a history of persecution. People most often greeted the commands and words of God with hostility, rejection, and anger. Why? Because God's words place demands on us, thwarting our autonomy and pretension. People would rather attack the messenger than heed the message. Death and imprisonment were the common lot of those who proclaimed God's word where it was not welcome (see, e.g., 2 Chron. 16:10; 18:25–26; 24:20–22; Mark 6:17–18; Luke 11:47–51; John 16:2; Acts 7:51–60; Rev. 18:24). In Elijah's day, many prophets were killed, others were hidden, and his own life was at risk. It would be the same when the last and greatest prophet appeared. When God at last sent his own Son, he also experienced the anger of a sinful world directed against a holy God (Matt. 21:33–41). Elijah was a man just like us (James 5:17); we, too, can share both in his boldness and in the opposition of a watching world. This sharing is the fellowship of the sufferings of Christ (Phil. 3:10; 1:29).

There are many possible responses to the difficulties of righteous living in a hostile world. On some occasions, withdrawal from the world and hiding may be an acceptable response (1 Kings 17:2; 18:4, 13). In the history of the church, the monastic movement and a series of Christian communes and settlements have tried forms of withdrawal. But Obadiah did not hide or withdraw. It was possible for him to serve God even as a minister in Ahab's government (1 Kings 18:3). Naaman could still receive God's blessing, even while standing in the temple of Rimmon (2 Kings 5:18–19). Daniel and his friends could serve Nebuchadnezzar, the king who had destroyed Jerusalem and deported the population. While Paul was persecuted and imprisoned in Rome, he was supported by "those who belong to Caesar's household" (Phil. 4:22; cf. 1:13).

Withdrawal may be in order for a time, whether to save lives or for spiritual refreshment. However, wholehearted engagement with the world, with the political and economic process, is for most of us the way in which we can bear witness before a watching world. Jesus did not pray that we be taken out of the world, but that we be protected from evil (John 17:15). Like the widow at Zarephath, Obadiah underwent the testing of his faith. His fears were well founded—Ahab might well have taken his life (1 Kings 18:14). But Obadiah was faithful, and God kept him from evil (cf. Matt. 6:13).

Elijah was about to enter into combat with evil single-handedly. The religious and political establishment was unanimously arrayed against him. The last and greatest prophet, Jesus, would also face such combat single-handedly. God would vindicate himself in both situations, in one by preserving the life of his servant, and in the other by accepting his death. When Jesus began to teach his disciples that he was going to die, he told them, "Whoever wants to save his life will lose it, but whoever loses his life for me and for the gospel will save it" (Mark 8:35). Elijah was unashamed of God's word, and the Son of Man will not be ashamed of him when he comes in his Father's glory (Mark 8:38). When John describes the defeat of the Evil One, he describes the church through the ages as having overcome him "by the blood of the Lamb and by the word of their testimony; they did not love their lives so much as to shrink from death" (Rev. 12:11). Few of us will ever face loss of life for the sake of the gospel—can we not be faithful in small things?

FOR FURTHER REFLECTION

1. Again (see chapter 2, section A, question 1) water plays a leading role in this story. What is the significance of water at the time of Elijah and Elisha?
2. Why was Ahab so perturbed by Elijah?
3. Our priorities ordinarily show up in high relief when there are not enough resources to go around. In the face of life-threatening drought and famine, where was Obadiah investing his resources? Ahab? How about you?
4. Try making a list with two columns. In the first column, list what you think should be your priorities. In the second column, use your calendar

and your checkbook to summarize how you actually spend your time and money. Do the two columns agree? What needs to change?

5. Obadiah was a man of great commitment and faith, but he also lived with a great fear of Ahab. Were his fears exaggerated? What fears keep you from obeying as you ought? Are they exaggerated, too?

B. IDOLATRY ON TRIAL
1 KINGS 18:16–46

So Obadiah went to meet Ahab and told him, and Ahab went to meet Elijah. When he saw Elijah, he said to him, "Is that you, you troubler of Israel?"

"I have not made trouble for Israel," Elijah replied. "But you and your father's family have. You have abandoned the LORD's commands and have followed the Baals. Now summon the people from all over Israel to meet me on Mount Carmel. And bring the four hundred and fifty prophets of Baal and the four hundred prophets of Asherah, who eat at Jezebel's table."

So Ahab sent word throughout all Israel and assembled the prophets on Mount Carmel. Elijah went before the people and said, "How long will you waver between two opinions? If the LORD is God, follow him; but if Baal is God, follow him."

But the people said nothing.

Then Elijah said to them, "I am the only one of the LORD's prophets left, but Baal has four hundred and fifty prophets. Get two bulls for us. Let them choose one for themselves, and let them cut it into pieces and put it on the wood but not set fire to it. I will prepare the other bull and put it on the wood but not set fire to it. Then you call on the name of your god, and I will call on the name of the Lord. The god who answers by fire—he is God."

Then all the people said, "What you say is good."

Elijah said to the prophets of Baal, "Choose one of the bulls and prepare it first, since there are so many of you. Call on the name of your god, but do not light the fire." So they took the bull given them and prepared it.

Then they called on the name of Baal from morning till noon. "O Baal, answer us!" they shouted. But there was no response; no one answered. And they danced around the altar they had made.

At noon Elijah began to taunt them. "Shout louder!" he said. "Surely he is a god! Perhaps he is deep in thought, or busy, or traveling. Maybe he is sleeping and must be awakened." So they shouted louder and slashed themselves with swords and spears, as was their custom, until their blood flowed. Midday passed, and they continued their frantic prophesying until the time for the evening sacrifice. But there was no response, no one answered, no one paid attention.

Then Elijah said to all the people, "Come here to me." They came to him, and he repaired the altar of the Lord, which was in ruins. Elijah took twelve stones, one for each of the tribes descended from Jacob, to whom the word of the Lord had come, saying, "Your name shall be Israel." With the stones he built an altar in the name of the Lord, and he dug a trench around it large enough to hold two seahs of seed. He arranged the wood, cut the bull into pieces and laid it on the wood. Then he said to them, "Fill four large jars with water and pour it on the offering and on the wood."

"Do it again," he said, and they did it again.

"Do it a third time," he ordered, and they did it the third time. The water ran down around the altar and even filled the trench.

At the time of sacrifice, the prophet Elijah stepped forward and prayed: "O Lord, God of Abraham, Isaac and Israel, let it be known today that you are God in Israel and that I am your servant and have done all these things at your command. Answer me, O Lord, answer me, so these people will know that you, O Lord, are God, and that you are turning their hearts back again."

Then the fire of the Lord fell and burned up the sacrifice, the wood, the stones and the soil, and also licked up the water in the trench.

When all the people saw this, they fell prostrate and cried, "The Lord—he is God! The Lord—he is God!"

Then Elijah commanded them, "Seize the prophets of Baal. Don't let anyone get away!" They seized them, and Elijah had them brought down to the Kishon Valley and slaughtered there.

And Elijah said to Ahab, "Go, eat and drink, for there is the sound of a heavy rain." So Ahab went off to eat and drink, but Elijah climbed to the top of Carmel, bent down to the ground and put his face between his knees.

"Go and look toward the sea," he told his servant. And he went up and looked.

"There is nothing there," he said.

Seven times Elijah said, "Go back."

The seventh time the servant reported, "A cloud as small as a man's hand is rising from the sea."

So Elijah said, "Go and tell Ahab, 'Hitch up your chariot and go down before the rain stops you.'"

Meanwhile, the sky grew black with clouds, the wind rose, a heavy rain came on and Ahab rode off to Jezreel. The power of the LORD came upon Elijah and, tucking his cloak into his belt, he ran ahead of Ahab all the way to Jezreel.

It was an uneven contest. The deck was stacked in favor of the prophets of Baal. Elijah summoned the people to Mount Carmel (1 Kings 18:19), which was located along the prominent range of rolling hills that formed the southern border of the plain of Jezreel. It rose about 1,800 feet above the surrounding plain and was situated near the shore of the Mediterranean Sea, above the modern port of Haifa. In the ninth century B.C., Mount Carmel marked the southern reaches of Phoenicia. As the highest point in the region, it was a desirable place to worship. Baalism was already strong there. Furthermore, the contest was staged in the particular area of Baal's power. In the art of ancient Syria, Baal was depicted holding a lightning bolt in his right hand; since he was the god of the storm, he should have easily been able to send a flash of lightning to ignite a sacrifice presented by his devotees. Let Baal bring the rain to end the drought and the lightning to start the fire. Not only was the contest held in Baal's territory, involving his specialty, but Baal also had the backing of the far greater number of supplicants and the support of the national leadership. The premise appeared to be that Baal would respond to volume. The Baal worshipers even had the greater amount of time; their caterwauling lasted from early morning to the time of the evening sacrifice (1 Kings 18:26–29). The king and 850 prophets (v. 19) would certainly catch his ear.

It was not just that Baal started with all the advantages, but Elijah started with a handicap that made God's task more difficult. Whereas the Baal cult on Carmel was well established, the altar to Yahweh had fallen into ruins (1 Kings 18:30). Even the offering and the firewood that Elijah had prepared were soaked with enough water to make a small moat at the base of the altar (vv. 33–35). Igniting this soggy array would be difficult indeed.

Every advantage that Baalism was given only served to increase the glory of the God who answered by fire. The greater the effort of the prophets of Baal was (1 Kings 18:26–29), the greater was their failure. The more Elijah taunted the fevered crowd calling on Baal, the more dismal Baal's performance became. The God who gives rain and answers by fire also rules over history in all of its small details and glorifies himself through them.

In our own lives, when circumstances seem overwhelming and the difficulties seem beyond our ability to overcome or even cope with, God then shows us his glory and power. God's power is shown most clearly in our weakness (1 Cor. 1:25, 27; 2 Cor. 12:7–9). Where our resources and efforts are insufficient, the glory and sufficiency of Christ shine ever so brightly.

There would be no room for compromise or negotiation. "Elijah, can't we serve both Baal and Yahweh?" No. "Well, can't we worship Yahweh most of the time, and just occasionally pay a bit of attention to Baal?" No. There can be no both-and in the service of Israel's God, only either-or. The first commandment demanded the exclusive loyalty of God's people (Ex. 20:3); he had redeemed them from bondage, and they were his (v. 2).

There is no room for double-mindedness here, no room to waver or doubt—not for Elijah, not for Israel, and not for you and me. They had been praying for rain and fire, but, as James would later warn, "a double-minded man" "should not think he will receive anything from the Lord" (James 1:7–8). No one can serve two masters (Matt. 6:24).

The idols of our day and society may not be images made of wood or stone. They are far more likely to be our own lusts or desires, money, power, position, security, and relationships. Perhaps the easiest way to identify our idols is to ask what we serve. Idols are often those things we are tempted to trust instead of God. What are those things for which we strive, those things we look to in order to achieve security or a sense of well-being? "Elijah, can't I serve God and Money?" No. "How about God and Job Success?" No. "Just a little?" No. There can be no wavering between two opinions. "If the LORD is God, follow him; but if Baal [or Money, or Power, or Security] is God, follow him" (1 Kings 18:21).

The rain would come again, just as Elijah had said. It would fall on the just and the unjust alike (Matt. 5:45). For all people serving idols, the rain is God's testimony to himself (Acts 14:17).

Mount Carmel overlooked the plain of Jezreel, quite near the ancient city of Megiddo in the plain below. The plain of Jezreel is perhaps the most contested piece of real estate in the history of the world. The major ancient highway linking three continents cut through a pass into the plain near Mount Carmel. Deborah, Joshua, David, Solomon, Josiah, the Philistines, the pharaohs of Egypt, the kings of Assyria, Babylon, and Persia, Alexander the Great, the Roman legions, the armies of Islam, the Crusaders, Napoleon, the Turks, the British, and the Israelis have all fought or otherwise sought to control this strategic highway through the plain of Jezreel. It is no surprise, then, that John describes the great apocalyptic battle as set at Armageddon, a Greek term meaning "mountain of Megiddo." That terrible final conflict between the armies of the God of heaven and the forces of evil is accompanied by a storm with flashes of lightning, rumbling peals of thunder, and huge hailstones (Rev. 16:16–21).

Elijah's confrontation with the prophets of Baal was a mini-enactment, an anticipation, of that great battle when God will intervene in history to vindicate his name completely and to eradicate idolatry from the world. After that confrontation, the people fell prostrate and cried out, "The LORD—he is God! The LORD—he is God!" (1 Kings 18:39).

Elijah ordered that the prophets of Baal be taken down to the Kishon Valley and slaughtered (1 Kings 18:40). The Kishon was the stream that drained the western end of the plain of Jezreel; it ran by Mount Carmel on the floor of the plain below. It was there that Sisera's chariots had bogged down in the mud (Judg. 4:15; 5:4–5, 19–22). It is no wonder, then, that Elijah told Ahab to set out in his chariot while he could still travel ahead of the coming rains (1 Kings 18:44).

Readers are occasionally uneasy with the slaughter of the prophets of Baal reported in this text. Keep in mind, however, that Elijah's battle points us toward the final conflict with evil. In the new Israel there is no place for idolatry (1 Cor. 6:9–10; Eph. 5:5; Rev. 21:8; 22:14–15). The utter defeat of evil—of all that sets itself up against God—is part of the goal of history. Elijah had but a foretaste. There remains "a fearful expectation of judgment and of raging fire that will consume the enemies of God" (Heb. 10:27). We live with the hope of someday seeing every knee bowed and every tongue confessing that Jesus Christ is Lord (Phil. 2:10–11).

What started out as a power struggle between Yahweh and Baal ended up as a burnt offering to Yahweh. God had in the past indicated his acceptance of an offering by an outbreak of fire that consumed it (Judg. 6:20–21; 1 Chron. 21:26). The fire that so often represents divine judgment becomes also a reminder of God's grace. He would accept a sacrifice for the sins of the people.

On another occasion, God delivered the decisive blow against evil and accepted a sacrifice for the sins of his people (1 Cor. 15:24–27; Heb. 10). The goal of the events at Mount Carmel was not so much judgment in the defeat of Baal as it was grace in reclaiming Israel (1 Kings 18:37).

With himself vindicated as a prophet, the offering consumed, the pagan priests slain, and God having promised that rain was on the way (1 Kings 18:1, 41), it was time for Elijah to kick back and take some time off. It was time to relax—right? Wrong. Elijah prayed that God would complete what he had begun (vv. 41–44). "Lord," he said, in effect, "you have shown that Baal is nothing, but now, O God, show yourself as the source of rain and life." Seven times Elijah prayed for rain, until a cloud was hovering on the horizon. James, who begins his book by urging us to persevere in prayer and warning us against double-mindedness (James 1:2–8), ends his book by reminding us of the effective and powerful prayer of Elijah (5:17–18). God will be true to his promises. How should we pray? "Lord, remember your promise." He who has begun a good work in you will carry it on to completion until the day of Christ Jesus (Phil. 1:6).

FOR FURTHER REFLECTION

1. How does knowledge of the religion of the Phoenician Baal throw light on this story?
2. God seems to fight pagan culture on its own ground. Is this an argument for addressing the culture in its own terms (see also Acts 17)? What would this look like today?

3. Since the fall of humankind into sin, the voice of righteousness in this wicked world has almost always been a minority opinion. The odds were overwhelming in Elijah's day. Yet generation after generation the power of God is revealed in the preaching of the gospel. What encouragement do you find in the story of Elijah and the prophets of Baal?

4. The slaughter of the prophets of Baal points toward the day when God will judge all sin; there will be no idolaters in his kingdom (1 Cor. 6:9; Rev. 21:8). God's servants should hate sin as much as God hates sin. But do we? What sorts of "little idols" are you soft on in your own life?

5. Both Elijah and Jesus displayed the power of God in their weakness when they confronted the hostility of the establishment. But they did it in very different ways. Where have you witnessed God's power shining brightly where you are weak?

4

THE FURTHER ADVENTURES OF ELIJAH, THE SERVANT OF THE LORD

First Kings 19 narrates two events in Elijah's life that immediately followed his triumph on Mount Carmel. At first we might expect that God's great victory over Baal (which was also Elijah's victory over Ahab) would have turned Israel in a new direction. But Ahab didn't repent; the people continued to reject God, and Elijah felt alone.

But, of course, he wasn't alone, and in these two stirring events God let him know that he was not without help. In the first section of 1 Kings 19, God speaks of those who will serve (and have already served) alongside Elijah. In the second section, we meet his closest helper, Elisha. The sections are verses 1–18 ("A Second Moses Visits God's Mountain") and verses 19–21 ("Elijah's Heir and Successor").

A. A SECOND MOSES VISITS GOD'S MOUNTAIN
1 KINGS 19:1–18

> Now Ahab told Jezebel everything Elijah had done and how he had killed all the prophets with

the sword. So Jezebel sent a messenger to Elijah to say, "May the gods deal with me, be it ever so severely, if by this time tomorrow I do not make your life like that of one of them."

Elijah was afraid and ran for his life. When he came to Beersheba in Judah, he left his servant there, while he himself went a day's journey into the desert. He came to a broom tree, sat down under it and prayed that he might die. "I have had enough, LORD," he said. "Take my life; I am no better than my ancestors." Then he lay down under the tree and fell asleep.

All at once an angel touched him and said, "Get up and eat." He looked around, and there by his head was a cake of bread baked over hot coals, and a jar of water. He ate and drank and then lay down again.

The angel of the LORD came back a second time and touched him and said, "Get up and eat, for the journey is too much for you." So he got up and ate and drank. Strengthened by that food, he traveled forty days and forty nights until he reached Horeb, the mountain of God. There he went into a cave and spent the night.

And the word of the LORD came to him: "What are you doing here, Elijah?"

He replied, "I have been very zealous for the LORD God Almighty. The Israelites have rejected your covenant, broken down your altars, and put your prophets to death with the sword. I am the only one left, and now they are trying to kill me too."

The LORD said, "Go out and stand on the mountain in the presence of the LORD, for the LORD is about to pass by."

Then a great and powerful wind tore the mountains apart and shattered the rocks before the LORD, but the LORD was not in the wind. After the wind there was an earthquake, but the LORD was not in the earthquake. After the earthquake came a fire, but the LORD was not in the fire. And after the fire came a gentle whisper. When Elijah heard it, he pulled his cloak over his face and went out and stood at the mouth of the cave.

Then a voice said to him, "What are you doing here, Elijah?"

He replied, "I have been very zealous for the LORD God Almighty. The Israelites have rejected your covenant, broken down your altars, and put your prophets to death with the sword. I am the only one left, and now they are trying to kill me too."

The LORD said to him, "Go back the way you came, and go to the Desert of Damascus. When you get there, anoint Hazael king over Aram. Also, anoint Jehu son of Nimshi king over Israel, and anoint Elisha son of Shaphat from Abel Meholah to succeed you as prophet. Jehu will put to death any who escape the sword of Hazael, and Elisha will put to death any who escape the sword of Jehu. Yet I reserve seven thousand in Israel—all whose knees have not bowed down to Baal and all whose mouths have not kissed him."

The gods of many nations, peoples, and cultures have been associated with mountains. In Canaanite mythology, Baal was depicted as living on a mountain in the north, a Mount Zaphon ("North Mountain," cf. Ps. 48:2). Even as far back as the Exodus, one locality was known by the name Baal Zephon, "Baal of the North" (Ex. 14:2, 9). It is striking that after the confrontation with the prophets of Baal, God took Elijah south, the opposite direction of Baal's dwelling, to the place where the nation of Israel was born when God entered into covenant with those who had left Egypt. It was in effect a geographic way of distancing Israel's faith from all that Baalism represented.

The prophet almost appears to have been caught off guard. Things weren't going the way he had hoped. After Carmel, shouldn't the nation have turned back to Yahweh *en masse?* Even Jezebel should have abandoned her pagan deities and turned to Yahweh, or at least the people should have risen up and removed Ahab and Jezebel from rule! But now the prophet was fleeing for his life again. What went wrong?

The display of raw power on Mount Carmel did not produce repentance in Jezebel (1 Kings 19:1–2). Instead, she renewed her effort to take the prophet's life. It should not come as a surprise that this was so. The crowds in Jesus' day saw his miracles and even heard the thunderous voice of God from heaven (John 12:28). Yet "even after Jesus had done all these miraculous signs in their presence, they still would not believe in him" (John 12:37). Jesus told a crowd of his countrymen that if they would not believe his word, "believe the miracles." But they still attempted to seize him (John 10:38–39). Deadened hearts and blinded eyes would not see or understand (Isa. 6:10). Miracles cannot of themselves soften hard hearts or open eyes—only God can do this.

The contest at Mount Carmel had come and gone, but evil remained. Elijah's victory there was not the definitive defeat of evil—that would only come later at a cross. The wheat and the weeds would continue to grow together (Matt. 13:24–30) until the great and final harvest.

The writer of Kings portrays this episode in Elijah's life so that it reflects the life of Moses. Moses had also experienced the power of God on a mountain, only to find idolatry under way when he came down (Ex. 32). Through

Moses, God had provided food and water for Israel during her forty years in the wilderness (Ex. 17; Num. 11; 20), and now he provides Elijah with food and water that will carry him for forty days (1 Kings 19:8). Moses had encountered God at Mount Sinai, and now God leads Elijah to that same place. There Elijah, like Moses, would experience the presence of God in the wind, earthquake, and fire (Ex. 19:16–19). The cave where Elijah took refuge (1 Kings 19:9) reminds us of the cleft in the rock that concealed Moses (Ex. 33:22). On that same mountain, God passed by both men (Ex. 33:19, 22; 1 Kings 19:11), and both avoided looking at God (Ex. 33:22–23; 1 Kings 19:13). Both were sent back to their tasks, their commissions to serve God renewed (Ex. 33:12–14; 1 Kings 19:15–16). Both Moses and Elijah complained that they had had enough and asked God to take their lives (Num. 11:15; 1 Kings 19:4; cf. Ex. 32:32), and God appointed prophets as help for each (Num. 11:16–17, 25; 1 Kings 19:16–17). Finally, both Moses and Elijah were the objects of God's special care at the time of their death (Deut. 34; 2 Kings 2).

Both Moses and Elijah would yet behold the glory of God and hear his voice at another time and on another mountain (Matt. 17:1–13). There the splendor of the Godhead enveloped Jesus, the Son of God, the one who was "the radiance of God's glory and the exact representation of his being" (Heb. 1:3). Of all the prophets through a millennium of Israel's history, only two had physically stood in the presence of the glory of God. Then they stood again in that presence when Christ was transfigured before them. Like Elijah, Jesus spent forty days in the wilderness (Matt. 4:2), but, unlike Elijah, he did not succumb to despair. All the Law and the Prophets testified of him (John 5:39; Luke 24:27).

Earthquake, storm, and fire (1 Kings 19:11–12) commonly announce the presence of God (a theophany) in the Old Testament. They are particularly associated with the appearance of the divine warrior in holy war against evil. It was Yahweh, the God of Israel, who made the clouds his chariot (Deut. 33:26; Pss. 68:4; 104:3; Isa. 19:1; Jer. 4:13; Ezek. 1). Baal was known in Canaanite mythology as the "rider of the clouds," but this epithet could properly belong only to the God of Israel. The heavens and the earth convulse at the appearance of the divine warrior.

Elijah was zealous for God, jealous for his glory (1 Kings 19:10, 14). No doubt he would have liked to see the divine warrior come in judgment against his enemies, to see God's vindication of himself on that great "day of the Lord." But it did not happen, and Elijah was left with a mixture of despondency, discouragement, defeat, and depression. "Lord, after Carmel, why stop now?"

God, in his mercy, gently rebuked his servant. The full repertoire of theophanic motifs paraded by the prophet one after the other, but God was not to be found in them. God was found instead in "a gentle whisper" (1 Kings 19:11–12).[1]

Just like the Jews of Jesus' day (1 Cor. 1:22), Christians in our own age often get caught up in looking for signs and wonders. Too often people want to nourish and sustain their faith through some ongoing encounter with the supranormal and miraculous, and when it does not come or occur, they sink into despondency. But God would continue to be present and to do his work at the time of Elijah through his gentle voice. Elijah would be joined by Elisha (1 Kings 19:16), and the work of God would go on even when Elijah was gone. The work and presence of God in Elijah's day, no less than in our own, were marked by the presence of the word of God. To a generation looking for signs, "we preach Christ," the wisdom and power of God (1 Cor. 1:18–31). It is his voice, God's word, that is powerful, sharper than a sword, judging the thoughts and attitudes of the heart, and laying all things bare before the eyes of God (Heb. 4:12–13). It is the gentle voice of God's Spirit that will "convict the world of guilt in regard to sin and righteousness and judgment" (John 16:8).

Elijah either overstated his case or he was mistaken. He complained to God that "I am the only one left" (1 Kings 19:10, 14). God assured the prophet that there were still seven thousand others in Israel who had not bowed down to Baal (v. 18). Elijah would not have to confront evil alone. Jehu would eliminate the dynasty of Ahab and Jezebel; Elisha would assist Elijah (vv. 16–17). Ultimately, faithful Israel—Israel that was without sin and had kept God's commands perfectly—would boil down to a remnant consisting of only one man. Jesus, as the embodiment of faithful Israel, would confront evil truly alone, forsaken even by God (Matt. 27:46). They would try to kill him, too (cf. 1 Kings 19:10, 14), and they would succeed. Neither Elijah nor Moses could give his life for the sins of Israel (Ex. 32:32; Num. 11:15; 1 Kings 19:4); only Jesus could do that.

The account of Jezebel is one of several occasions in the Bible where a woman is portrayed as the embodiment of evil. Other examples would include her relative, Athaliah (2 Kings 11; 2 Chron. 22:10–23:21), Dame Folly (Prov. 5–7), and Herodias (Matt. 14:1–12). The feminist movement has informed us that such passages can be taken as offensive by women. Yet it must be remembered that many men are also portrayed as the embodiment of evil in the Bible (Ahab, Manasseh, Ahaz, and others). Many women are also depicted as the embodiment of virtue. For every Jezebel, there is a Deborah; for every Athaliah, a Ruth or Esther; for every Herodias, a Mary; for Dame Folly, Dame Wisdom (Prov. 8).

Yet in reading about Jezebel, one cannot but think of Babylon, the great whore (Rev. 17). Like Jezebel, she was drunk with the blood of those who bore witness for God (Rev. 17:6) and made war against his people (Rev. 17:14); but, like Jezebel of old (2 Kings 9:30–37), she will be brought to ruin.

Things looked bleak to Elijah. Even after the victory on Mount Carmel, it appeared that Baalism might yet triumph in Israel. The altars to Yahweh were in ruin; his prophets had been hunted down and murdered. Had God rejected his people? Had he forsaken them?

But Elijah could not see the whole picture. God assured the prophet that there was still a faithful remnant in Israel. Even in this time of extraordinary apostasy, God had preserved a faithful people.

Centuries later, Paul would reflect on 1 Kings 19:18. The seven thousand who were faithful were for Paul an argument that God had not rejected his people then, and that in his own day God had preserved a remnant for himself, chosen and saved by his grace, not by works (Rom. 11:1–6).

FOR FURTHER REFLECTION

1. Moses, Elijah, and Jesus were the great prophets of Israel. How were their lives alike? How were they different? What recurring themes unify the lives and experiences of God's prophets?
2. It seems that often in American Christianity, especially in the preaching of some televangelists, faithfulness to God is supposed to issue in a trouble-free life. But friendship with God more often than not means being at odds with a sinful world. Opposition and sometimes discouragement result. Have you ever experienced this?

3. How do the events on the Mount of Transfiguration testify to the deity of Jesus?
4. The hiding of Moses and Elijah from exposure to the divine presence on Mount Sinai was the inspiration for the famous hymn "Rock of Ages." Here are some other passages in the Old Testament that speak of a special rock: Exodus 17:1–7; Numbers 20:1–13; Deuteronomy 32:4; Psalms 19:14; 118:22; Isaiah 8:14; 26:4; 28:16; 51:1; Daniel 2:34; Zechariah 3:9; 4:7. How do the New Testament writers develop this theme (see Rom. 9:33; 1 Cor. 10:4; 1 Peter 2:8)?
5. Even after the contest on Mount Carmel, evil remained. After Jesus died and was raised, evil remained. When, according to the Bible, will it all end?

B. ELIJAH'S HEIR AND SUCCESSOR
1 KINGS 19:19–21

So Elijah went from there and found Elisha son of Shaphat. He was plowing with twelve yoke of oxen, and he himself was driving the twelfth pair. Elijah went up to him and threw his cloak around him. Elisha then left his oxen and ran after Elijah. "Let me kiss my father and mother good-by," he said, "and then I will come with you."

"Go back," Elijah replied. "What have I done to you?"

So Elisha left him and went back. He took his yoke of oxen and slaughtered them. He burned the plowing equipment to cook the meat and gave it to the people, and they ate. Then he set out to follow Elijah and became his attendant.

Alongside the ongoing succession of kings in both Israel and Judah, God had provided a parallel ongoing succession of prophets to bear witness to his word. The prophets were the successors of Moses (Deut. 18:14–22). Almost every king in the history of the two kingdoms would have his prophetic conscience; the prophets called upon the rulers of Israel to rule in accordance with the law of God (Deut. 17:18–19). Occasionally a son would take up the prophetic vocation of his father. In this instance, Elisha became in effect the spiritual son of Elijah. Just as God sent Elijah to inaugurate the next ruling dynasty, so also the prophet anointed his own successor (1 Kings 19:16–17).

God would not leave himself without a witness. In each generation, there would be those to guide the nation in the way of truth. The writer of Hebrews understood this and gave to the infant church a history of those who had made a good confession before a watching world (Heb. 11). The implications of that history for the church were also stated:

> Therefore, since we are surrounded by such a great cloud of witnesses, let us throw off everything that hinders and the sin that so easily entangles, and let us run with perseverance the race marked out for us. Let us fix our eyes on Jesus, the author and perfecter of our faith, who for the joy set before him endured the cross, scorning its shame, and sat down at the right hand of the throne of God. Consider him who endured such opposition from sinful men, so that you will not grow weary and lose heart. (Heb. 12:1–3)

In the Old Testament, the Spirit of God most often appears as the Spirit that empowers and enables prophecy. Many passages associate the gift of prophecy with possession of the Spirit (e.g., Num. 11:25–26, 29; 1 Sam. 10:6, 10; 1 Kings 22:22–23; 2 Kings 2:15; Joel 2:28; Zech. 7:12; cf. Luke 1:67; Acts 2:17–18). One way in which the writers of the Old Testament described possession by God's Spirit was to say that the Spirit "clothed" a prophet (1 Chron. 12:18–19; 2 Chron. 24:20; Judg. 6:34). This is the background for the symbolism involved when Elijah cast his cloak around Elisha (1 Kings 19:19). Elisha, like Elijah, would be clothed with the Spirit of God, inducted into the order of the prophets. Later, when Elijah was taken into heaven, Elisha picked up the cloak of Elijah and divided the Jordan; then the company of prophets knew that "the spirit of Elijah is resting on Elisha" (2 Kings 2:13–15).

Moses had centuries before declared, "I wish that all the LORD's people were prophets and that the LORD would put his Spirit on them!" (Num. 11:29). Almost a millennium later, Joel foresaw a day when God would grant Moses' wish and pour out his Spirit on his people (Joel 2:28–29).[2] The apostles on the day of Pentecost appealed to Joel to explain what was happening to the church on that grand day (Acts 2:16–18). In the church, God's Spirit was not the province of the few, but was poured out on all, and so all Christians have been given a prophetic function of bearing witness for God in their generation.

The Old Testament usage underlies much of the New Testament language that associates clothing imagery with possession by God's Spirit or being in Christ. We, too, have been clothed with the Spirit of God, the Spirit of Christ. The clothing of God's Spirit is the guarantee that we will be clothed with the resurrection body, our spiritual body (1 Cor. 15:53–54; 2 Cor. 5:2–5). We are to put off the old self and put on the new (Col. 3:9–10), to clothe ourselves with Christ (Rom. 13:14; Gal. 3:27). We, too, wear the prophet's mantle and bear witness for God in our generation.

The rains had come after the humiliation of Baal on Mount Carmel, and now Elisha was out plowing the softened ground. Standing behind a twelve-pair team of oxen, Elisha must have belonged to a wealthy family and been a formidable figure. Yet when called by God, he turned his team and the wooden implements of his trade into a fellowship offering enjoyed by all (cf. 2 Sam. 24:22, 25). There would be no going back for Elisha. Just as the disciples abruptly left their nets (Matt. 4:21–22; cf. 9:9), so Elijah burned his bridges behind him. He was doing what the writer of Hebrews later urged the church to do: to throw aside everything that might hinder or entangle him (Heb. 12:1). There was a new race to run, a new field to plow. There would be no holding of the new life in one hand and of the old life in the other.

Elijah's response to Elisha's inquiry about bidding farewell to his parents is somewhat enigmatic: "What have I done to you?" (1 Kings 19:20). Some see skepticism on Elijah's part; others, restraint that said in effect, "Make your own decision." The decision was not between Elijah and Elisha, but between Elisha and God (cf. John 2:4). The text does not explicitly indicate whether Elisha said farewell to his parents, although the communal feast from the slain oxen does imply that he did.

The Jews of Jesus' day would have recognized immediately that Jesus was alluding to this passage in Luke 9:57–62. When a would-be follower of Jesus said, "I will follow you, Lord; but first let me go back and say goodby to my family" (v. 61), Jesus replied, "No one who puts his hand to the plow and looks back is fit for service in the kingdom of God" (v. 62). The cost of following God is the same in both the Old and the New Testaments. It is to be single-minded. As DeVries observes, if you are not ready for this kind of commitment, you had better stay home with the oxen.[3] One greater than Elijah has come, and his call is even more demanding: "If anyone comes to me and does not hate his father and mother, his wife and children, his brothers and sisters—yes, even his own life—he cannot be my disciple. And anyone who does not carry his cross and follow me cannot be my disciple" (Luke 14:26–27).[4]

Do not overlook the divine initiative in Elisha's call. God had already chosen the prophet before the call was presented to him (1 Kings 19:16). It is ever true that "we love because he first loved us" (1 John 4:19).

FOR FURTHER REFLECTION

1. As those possessed by the Spirit of Christ, all Christians have the prophetic duty to bear witness in their generation. How are you meeting this responsibility? Remember that God has not given us a spirit of timidity, but of power (2 Tim. 1:7).
2. God's call to all of us is to single-mindedness and commitment. For some, that means leaving one's trade or business to pursue a professional vocation in ministry. For others, that means dedicated service in many different endeavors. Whatever our work, whether in ministry or other employment, God's call to service and commitment must eclipse all others. How are you responding to that call?
3. In this story, is God calling us to abandon our loved ones in order to serve him? In what sense?
4. This episode teaches us that there is a succession of prophets who served as God's servants. Who are prophets today—and in what sense?
5. Elisha received God's call to ministry and responded. Are only prophets and ministers called by God to service? Do you have a sense of calling in your present vocation?

5

ELIJAH VERSUS THE KINGS

One important task of a prophet was to serve as the conscience of the king. In better times, we had the relationship between Samuel and Saul and between Nathan and David. The kings sinned and sometimes did not fully repent, but at least they listened and allowed the prophets into their presence.

The following two accounts tell a different story. No love is lost between Elijah and Ahab; we have already seen this. But in 1 Kings 21, the story of Naboth's field, it reaches a climax. Even though the prophet is not present at the death of the king (see 1 Kings 22), at the end of 1 Kings 21 we hear Elijah pronounce God's sentence of death upon him.

The situation does not improve with Ahaziah (2 Kings 1), Ahab's son. His story lasts barely a chapter. As with Ahab, the prophet announces this king's death sentence on account of his sins.

A. "NEW LAMPS FOR OLD"
1 KINGS 21

Some time later there was an incident involving a vineyard belonging to Naboth the Jezreelite. The vineyard was in Jezreel, close to the palace of

Ahab king of Samaria. Ahab said to Naboth, "Let me have your vineyard to use for a vegetable garden, since it is close to my palace. In exchange I will give you a better vineyard or, if you prefer, I will pay you whatever it is worth."

But Naboth replied, "The LORD forbid that I should give you the inheritance of my fathers."

So Ahab went home, sullen and angry because Naboth the Jezreelite had said, "I will not give you the inheritance of my fathers." He lay on his bed sulking and refused to eat.

His wife Jezebel came in and asked him, "Why are you so sullen? Why won't you eat?"

He answered her, "Because I said to Naboth the Jezreelite, 'Sell me your vineyard; or if you prefer, I will give you another vineyard in its place.' But he said, 'I will not give you my vineyard.'"

Jezebel his wife said, "Is this how you act as king over Israel? Get up and eat! Cheer up. I'll get you the vineyard of Naboth the Jezreelite."

So she wrote letters in Ahab's name, placed his seal on them, and sent them to the elders and nobles who lived in Naboth's city with him. In those letters she wrote:

> "Proclaim a day of fasting and seat Naboth in a prominent place among the people. But seat two scoundrels opposite him and have them testify that he has cursed both God and the king. Then take him out and stone him to death."

So the elders and nobles who lived in Naboth's city did as Jezebel directed in the letters she had written to them. They proclaimed a fast and seated Naboth in a prominent place among the people. Then two scoundrels came and sat opposite him and brought charges against Naboth before the people, saying, "Naboth has cursed both God and the king." So they took him outside the city and stoned him to death. Then they sent word to Jezebel: "Naboth has been stoned and is dead."

As soon as Jezebel heard that Naboth had been stoned to death, she said to Ahab, "Get up and take possession of the vineyard of Naboth the Jezreelite that he refused to sell you. He is no longer alive, but dead." When Ahab heard that Naboth was dead, he got up and went down to take possession of Naboth's vineyard.

Then the word of the LORD came to Elijah the Tishbite: "Go down to meet Ahab king of Israel, who rules in Samaria. He is now in Naboth's vineyard, where he has gone to take possession of it. Say to him, 'This is what the LORD says: Have you not murdered a man and seized his property?' Then say to him, 'This is what the LORD says: In the place where dogs licked up Naboth's blood, dogs will lick up your blood— yes, yours!'"

Ahab said to Elijah, "So you have found me, my enemy!"

"I have found you," he answered, "because you have sold yourself to do evil in the eyes of the LORD. 'I am going to bring disaster on you. I will consume your descendants and cut off from Ahab every last male in Israel—slave or free. I will make your house like that of Jeroboam son of Nebat and that of Baasha son of Ahijah, because you have provoked me to anger and have caused Israel to sin.'

"And also concerning Jezebel the LORD says: 'Dogs will devour Jezebel by the wall of Jezreel.'

"Dogs will eat those belonging to Ahab who die in the city, and the birds of the air will feed on those who die in the country."

(There was never a man like Ahab, who sold himself to do evil in the eyes of the LORD, urged on by Jezebel his wife. He behaved in the vilest manner by going after idols, like the Amorites the LORD drove out before Israel.)

When Ahab heard these words, he tore his clothes, put on sackcloth and fasted. He lay in sackcloth and went around meekly.

Then the word of the LORD came to Elijah the Tishbite: "Have you noticed how Ahab has humbled himself before me? Because he has humbled himself, I will not bring this disaster in his day, but I will bring it on his house in the days of his son."

Almost every child is familiar with the story of Aladdin's lamp from *A Thousand and One Nights.* One character looking for the magic lamp goes through the streets crying out, "New lamps for old!" It is an effective ploy in the story about Aladdin. It is not unlike the approach that Ahab took to Naboth. Looking at it from Naboth's vantage point, there was much to commend the deal (1 Kings 21:2). The expansion of the royal palace was driving up the land values around it. Naboth would have an even better vineyard or could ask for an inflated price; it was also an opportunity to curry royal favor for himself and his family. Who wouldn't take a deal like this? There was everything to gain, and the offer did not appear to have a downside.

To understand why Naboth refused the offer (1 Kings 21:3), we have to understand what the land represented in Israel. God had promised to Abraham and his descendants that they would occupy the region after four hundred years of servitude. When God redeemed his people, he would not just bring them out of bondage (Gen. 15:14, 16), he would also bring them into an inheritance, the land he had promised (v. 18). Redemption for Israel was not simply escape from slavery to a foreign power, but also provision for the future. The Exodus and the Conquest together formed part of a single redemptive act. The promise of God to the fathers was not realized when the nation left Egypt, but only when it possessed its inheritance in the land.

Because the land represented the fruit of the nation's redemption, God commanded that it remain in the hands of the families to whom it was originally allotted. The land had been provided by God as part of his grace toward Israel; therefore, no one was to take the land of another away from him. The law provided that the land could be leased for a period, but that it could never be sold outright (Lev. 25:13–17, 25–28). No one would be deprived of the inheritance God had provided for him in the redemption of Israel. Since the land came to Israel as the result of the redemptive act of God, the land itself belonged to God, and provision always had to be made for the redemption of the land so that it returned to the ownership of the original family (Lev. 25:23–24). Naboth spoke the truth when he replied to Ahab, "The LORD forbid that I should give you the inheritance of my fathers" (1 Kings 21:3).

The New Testament uses Israel's experience as representative of the redemption that Christ has provided for the church. Jesus redeems us from bondage to a foreign power; he frees us from the dominion of Satan and slavery to sin (Heb. 2:14–15). But the redemption provided by Christ does not end with freedom from bondage; it also includes the provision of an inheritance that comes as the fruit of our redemption. But appreciate the difference between the New Testament and the Old. Whereas Naboth's inheritance could be taken from him forcibly by vile and violent men, the inheritance that Christ has provided is "an inheritance that can never perish, spoil or fade—kept in heaven for you, who through faith are shielded by God's power" (1 Peter 1:4–5). Moth and rust cannot destroy it, and thieves cannot break in to steal (Matt. 6:19–20). From the vantage point of the New Testament, the promises of God to Israel were shadows pointing toward an even greater inheritance in Christ.

So many in our own day have no inheritance, treasure, or possession that transcends the grave. Lives are poured out on the altar of materialism, even though no one has ever seen an armored truck following the hearse in a funeral procession. Jesus urges us, "Store up for yourselves treasures in heaven . . . for where your treasure is, there your heart will be also" (Matt. 6:20–21).

One might wish that Naboth's fidelity to God's command triumphed over Ahab's wishes. But not every instance of fidelity is greeted with the experience that Elijah had on Mount Carmel. Otherwise there would never have been a murdered prophet or a martyr. Living by the law of God in a lawless world provokes hostility. "In this world you will have trouble. But take heart! I have overcome the world" (John 16:33). Even the sinless Son of God was greeted with such anger and was put to death.

The picture of Ahab moping around the palace like a disconsolate, spoiled child makes a sorry sight indeed (1 Kings 21:4). Samuel had warned Israel that the kingship they desired would go awry, and that the king would "take the best of your fields and vineyards and olive groves" (1 Sam. 8:14). Kingship would become corrupt, until the people cried out for relief (v. 18).

Ahab's appetites and weakness provided an opportunity for Jezebel to assert herself forcefully. Her devotion to Baal did not restrain her from hiring false witnesses to accuse Naboth of treason and blasphemy (1 Kings 21:9–13). False religion often goes hand in glove with oppression and violence, injustice and crime. The same charges would later be leveled by false witnesses against Jesus in his trial (Matt. 26:59–66; Mark 14:55–64).

God is a revealer of secrets (Dan. 2:28–30). He sent Elijah to meet Ahab at the scene of the crime (1 Kings 21:17–18). Ahab would not have time to enjoy his ill-gotten vineyard before hearing that he and Jezebel would become dog food on Naboth's land (vv. 19, 23). Ahab had a foretaste of the day "when God will judge men's secrets" (Rom. 2:16). "Nothing in all creation is hidden from God's sight. Everything is uncovered and laid bare before the eyes of him to whom we must give account" (Heb. 4:13). The psalmist describes as fools those who think that the Lord does not see or hear (Ps. 94:7). Could it be that he who implanted the ear does not hear, or that he who formed the eye does not see (Ps. 94:9)? A corrupt throne may ally itself with evil and condemn the innocent to death, but God "will repay them for their sins and destroy them for their wickedness" (Ps. 94:20–23).

The prophets often confronted the kings of Israel and Judah after their transgressions (2 Sam. 12; 1 Kings 20:37–43; 2 Kings 20:16–18). The statement that dogs would devour a king became almost a formulaic announcement of the end of a dynasty (1 Kings 14:11; 16:4; 22:38; 2 Kings 9:10, 36). Israel had to keep looking for a faithful king who would rule with righteousness and justice, in accord with all of God's commandments, until "the kingdom of the world has become the kingdom of our Lord and of his Christ, and he will reign for ever and ever" (Rev. 11:15).

The attitude of the writer of Kings toward Ahab is almost uniformly negative. Ahab considered sin to be trivial and did more evil than all the kings before him (1 Kings

16:31, 33). He sold himself to do evil and behaved in the vilest manner (21:20, 25).

Yet even Ahab could respond to the word of God. This chief of sinners humbled himself and was contrite (1 Kings 21:27). God was pleased with the repentance of Ahab, and because of this repentance, forestalled the judgment announced against him (v. 28). The words of Ezekiel are as relevant in our own generation as they would have been for Ahab: "As surely as I live, declares the Sovereign LORD, I take no pleasure in the death of the wicked, but rather that they turn from their ways and live" (Ezek. 33:11; cf. 18:23). God wants to see the repentance and contrition of Ahabs like you and me. There is rejoicing in heaven over the one who repents, not over the ninety-nine who do not see the need (Luke 15:7, 10).

FOR FURTHER REFLECTION

1. It is human nature always to want more. Reflect on your own desires. What means are you tempted to employ to get what you want in life?
2. The inheritance we have in Christ is imperishable and cannot be taken from us. But sometimes we fall for the ploy of taking the new lamps for the old. The temptation there is to exchange our glorious God for a grass-eating bull (Ps. 106:20). The world constantly dangles attractive trinkets before us. It is easy to want more than we have—houses, trips, furniture, cars, clothes—the list is endless. It is no wonder that Paul tells us that "godliness with contentment is great gain" (1 Tim. 6:6). When we are discontented, what are we saying to God about what he has done for us? Where does discontent lead?
3. Many in American society have just about all the world has to offer, but they are impoverished

when it comes to heaven's inexhaustible riches. Have you spoken recently with some needy soul about the riches in Christ Jesus?

4. Obedience to God can sometimes end in tragedy. Naboth chose to obey, even at the cost of his life. But God will not let violence done to his people go unpunished—he will judge those who trample upon the upright. "'It is mine to avenge; I will repay,' says the Lord" (Rom. 12:19, quoting Deut. 32:35). Have you learned, when you are wronged, to leave vengeance with God?

5. Where do righteous people like Naboth get their reward—or does the story end for Naboth with his unjust death?

B. THE SINS OF THE FATHER
2 KINGS 1

After Ahab's death, Moab rebelled against Israel. Now Ahaziah had fallen through the lattice of his upper room in Samaria and injured himself. So he sent messengers, saying to them, "Go and consult Baal-Zebub, the god of Ekron, to see if I will recover from this injury."

But the angel of the LORD said to Elijah the Tishbite, "Go up and meet the messengers of the king of Samaria and ask them, 'Is it because there is no God in Israel that you are going off to consult Baal-Zebub, the god of Ekron?' Therefore this is what the LORD says: 'You will not leave the bed you are lying on. You will certainly die!'" So Elijah went.

When the messengers returned to the king, he asked them, "Why have you come back?"

"A man came to meet us," they replied. "And he said to us, 'Go back to the king who sent you and tell him, "This is what the LORD says: Is it because there is no God in Israel that you are sending men to consult Baal-Zebub, the god of Ekron? Therefore you will not leave the bed you are lying on. You will certainly die!"'"

The king asked them, "What kind of man was it who came to meet you and told you this?"

They replied, "He was a man with a garment of hair and with a leather belt around his waist."

The king said, "That was Elijah the Tishbite."

Then he sent to Elijah a captain with his company of fifty men. The captain went up to Elijah, who was sitting on the top of a hill, and said to him, "Man of God, the king says, 'Come down!'"

Elijah answered the captain, "If I am a man of God, may fire come down from heaven and consume you and your fifty men!" Then fire fell from heaven and consumed the captain and his men.

At this the king sent to Elijah another captain with his fifty men. The captain said to him, "Man of God, this is what the king says, 'Come down at once!'"

"If I am a man of God," Elijah replied, "may fire come down from heaven and consume you and your fifty men!" Then the fire of God fell from heaven and consumed him and his fifty men.

So the king sent a third captain with his fifty men. This third captain went up and fell on his knees before Elijah. "Man of God," he begged, "please have respect for my life and the lives of these fifty men, your servants! See, fire has fallen from heaven and consumed the first two captains and all their men. But now have respect for my life!"

The angel of the LORD said to Elijah, "Go down with him; do not be afraid of him." So Elijah got up and went down with him to the king.

He told the king, "This is what the LORD says: Is it because there is no God in Israel for you to consult that you have sent messengers to consult Baal-Zebub, the god of Ekron? Because you have done this, you will never leave the bed you are lying on. You will certainly die!" So he died, according to the word of the LORD that Elijah had spoken.

Because Ahaziah had no son, Joram succeeded him as king in the second year of Jehoram son of Jehoshaphat king of Judah. As for all the other events of Ahaziah's reign, and what he did, are they not written in the book of the annals of the kings of Israel?

After the death of Ahab during the battle of Ramoth Gilead (1 Kings 22), Ahaziah attained the throne of Israel. Ahaziah was the son of Ahab and Jezebel, so it comes as no surprise to hear that "he did evil in the eyes of the LORD, because he walked in the ways of his father and mother . . . he served and worshiped Baal and provoked the LORD, the God of Israel, to anger, just as his father had done" (22:51–53). Although he should already have learned from events during the reign of his parents, Ahaziah had to learn for himself how impotent Baal was. The very fact that Ahaziah sought a Baal outside the land of Israel could be testimony to the effectiveness of Elijah's actions in curbing the Baal cult (18:40). But this time, since the son refused to learn from the experience of his parents, the stakes were higher and the results were more drastic: when the fire fell, it did not fall on an offering on an altar as at Carmel (v. 38), but rather on the soldiers and messengers of the king (2 Kings 1:10, 12). The immolation of the first group of fifty should have been enough to convince the king, but like the pharaoh of the Exodus, his heart was hard, and he would not learn.

At base, there is always an element of irrationality in sin. Sin is not simply rebellion. It is foolish, stupid, and wrongheaded—the product of poor reasoning. Any king of Israel should have remembered the itinerary of the ark of the covenant among the city-states of the Philistines. When the ark came to Ekron, the inhabitants were afflicted with horrible tumors, and panic spread through the city (1 Sam. 5:10–12). The Philistine gods could not stand in the presence of the ark and could not sustain the health and well-being of the population (1 Sam. 5). Why then would anyone go to the god of Ekron to find an answer to a question about his health (2 Kings 1:2)? Didn't the history of Israel already contain eloquent testimony to the foolishness of such a move?

Human beings seek relief from the chaos and the vagaries of life; they strive endlessly to be masters of their own destiny to whatever degree possible. They will turn in almost any direction and pursue any religious cult or philosophical movement that promises to relieve the terror of the unknown. Sadly, like Ahaziah, they will seek almost anything but the Lord. The Scriptures regularly exhort us to call out to God, to seek him while he may be found. How foolish it is to fall for the counterfeits! And how foolish it was for Israel or is for us to have "exchanged their Glory" for idols (Ps. 106:20; cf. Rom. 1:23).

There is another exchange in this story. Ahaziah was seeking an oracle from Baal-Zebub (2 Kings 1:2). Although the issue is debatable, the ancient scribes appear to have had a bit of fun with the name of this god. "Baal-Zebub" means literally "lord of a fly"—not exactly what we would regard as a flattering name for a deity. It is more probable that the original name was "Baal-Zebul," which would mean "Prince Baal" or "glorious Baal." At Ugarit, Baal was known as "the Prince, the lord of the earth." By exchanging one letter for another (the final *l* for a *b*), the scribes may have deliberately and pejoratively distorted the god's true name both as a source of humor and as a way of stating their own estimate of this deity's worth. The New Testament may preserve the vestiges of the original name in the term *Beelzebul,* a designation for the chief of devils (Matt. 10:25; 12:24, 27; Mark 3:22; Luke 11:15, 18–19); the Vulgate associates this term with the designation for the god of Ekron in 2 Kings 1:2 and reads "Beelzebub."

Whether the scribes were deliberately tarnishing the reputation of Baal by tinkering with his name or not, the narrative itself does a thorough job of deprecating the Baal of Ekron. Recall that Baal was the lord of fire and lightning. When Ahaziah sought Baal, it was Yahweh who responded by showing his dominion in the area that was supposedly Baal's forte. Fire fell as it had at Carmel, but it fell on those seeking Baal. As a god who returned annually from the dead and gave fertility to the earth, Baal was looked to for healing and restoration to life from threatening illness. But no matter what oracle Ahaziah may have received from the Baal of Ekron, Yahweh had already pronounced his verdict, and the king would not recover from his fall. Whatever might be learned from the Baal of Ekron was irrelevant. "The Most High . . . does as he pleases with the powers of heaven and the peoples of the earth. No one can hold back his hand" (Dan. 4:34–35).

Various commentators have found Elijah's actions foolish or calloused, out of accord with God's true nature. For many modern readers, the prophet appears almost flippant or casual in the way he calls down fire on the messengers instead of on the king; a group of potentially innocent garrison soldiers are reduced to ashes instead of the king who sent them. Rather, shouldn't we come to grips with the fact that our God is a consuming fire (Heb. 12:29; Deut. 4:24), who demands that he be worshiped with reverence and awe (Heb. 12:28)?

The God of the Bible will not tolerate hubris. Human pride and pretentiousness draw an unremitting response of judgment and anger from God. In ancient Israel, a messenger ordinarily introduced his message with the phrase "Thus says X" or "X says," and then proceeded to speak as if he were the sending person. Ahaziah's messengers came and said, "The king says . . ." so that the following imperative, "Come down!" was the command of the king, not of the messenger (2 Kings 1:9, 11). The messenger had the authority of the one who sent him. Ahaziah's first messenger said, "Come down." But instead of learning from the experience of the first group, the king became even more demanding through the second messenger: "Come down at once!" The problem here was that the prophet was the messenger of God. Just as Ahaziah's messengers enjoyed the power and respect due to their king, so too Elijah commanded the respect and reverence due to the One who sent him. The king was about to learn that no one could command God (Isa. 40:13–14). Although the first two groups addressed the prophet as "man of God," they mistakenly assumed that he could still be coerced.

Because the third messenger did not speak with the imperiousness and arrogance of the king, he and his troops were spared. The king in his pride refused to seek God for information about his life, but the third captain bowed before the prophet. This captain's approach showed reverence for the Lord; his life and the life of his men would be spared, but the life of the king would end. He recognized correctly that it was not the life of the prophet that was at risk, but his own life and that of his men.

One can only wonder why the king insisted that the prophet come to him personally. He would take the word of a messenger about the oracle from the Baal of Ekron (2 Kings 1:2), and it was a messenger who brought him the word of Yahweh that he would die (v. 4). Did he really think he could intimidate the prophet and change the verdict of God? When the prophet did appear before the king, the verdict remained the same (v. 16). The words of a true prophet come to pass, and Ahaziah did indeed die (v. 17). The pretentiousness that had set itself up against God was demolished (2 Cor. 10:5).

John the Baptist foretold that the one who followed him would baptize with Spirit and fire (Matt. 3:11; Luke 3:16). Ahaziah's messengers had come from Samaria (2 Kings 1:1). When Jesus' disciples were rejected by a Samaritan village, they predictably asked, "Lord, do you want us to call fire down from heaven to destroy them?" (Luke 9:53–54). But vengeance belongs to the Lord (Rom. 12:19; Deut. 32:35).

There was another day when a faithful messenger came from God. He was God's own Son, and he was worthy of the reverence and devotion of all people. Yet there he hung on a cross, and Elijah did not come with fire to rescue him (Matt. 27:47–49; Mark 15:35–36). Instead, Jesus humbled himself and endured the fiery indignation of God in order that we might have life. And now the church in his name calls on all people to humble themselves and bow down before him. Where pride remains too strong and people will not reverence and worship Jesus Christ, there remains only "a fearful expectation of judgment and of raging fire that will consume the enemies of God" (Heb. 10:27). We know him who said, "It is mine to avenge; I will repay"; it is "a dreadful thing to fall into the hands of the living God" (Heb. 10:30–31). It is only because Jesus has interposed himself between us and God that the death sentence pronounced against us (2 Cor. 1:9) is revoked.

FOR FURTHER REFLECTION

1. Ahaziah fell ill and his first thought for help was not the Lord, but an idol. When crisis strikes our life, where do we turn first for help?
2. Ahaziah followed in his father's footsteps. Like father, like son. Is it fair to judge someone whose environment or upbringing has contributed to his evil behavior?
3. A hundred men died because of Ahaziah's sin. Our sins always affect other people. Think of ways in which your sins affect others. Who is going to be hurt because of your transgression? What kind of example do you set for others?
4. Was it just for the prophet to call fire down on the heads of the messengers? Why or why not?
5. While the first two messengers followed Ahaziah in his pride and arrogance, the third captain in effect asked for mercy from God by asking it from Elijah. Think about what it means to approach God humbly, renouncing our pride and asking for mercy.

I Tim 6:6

6

ELISHA SUCCEEDS ELIJAH

Elijah served the Lord well. He had his moments of doubt and self-pity, but he also stood up courageously on God's behalf in dangerous times. His time for rest arrived and his successor was in the wings.

In the next two sections (2 Kings 2), Elisha is initiated as Elijah's successor and begins his ministry. Elijah may be gone, but God's power to resist evil continues through Elisha.

A. PASSING THE MANTLE
2 KINGS 2:1–18

When the LORD was about to take Elijah up to heaven in a whirlwind, Elijah and Elisha were on their way from Gilgal. Elijah said to Elisha, "Stay here; the LORD has sent me to Bethel."

But Elisha said, "As surely as the LORD lives and as you live, I will not leave you." So they went down to Bethel.

The company of the prophets at Bethel came out to Elisha and asked, "Do you know that the LORD is going to take your master from you today?"

"Yes, I know," Elisha replied, "but do not speak of it."

Then Elijah said to him, "Stay here, Elisha; the LORD has sent me to Jericho."

And he replied, "As surely as the LORD lives and as you live, I will not leave you." So they went to Jericho.

The company of the prophets at Jericho went up to Elisha and asked him, "Do you know that the LORD is going to take your master from you today?"

"Yes, I know," he replied, "but do not speak of it."

Then Elijah said to him, "Stay here; the LORD has sent me to the Jordan."

And he replied, "As surely as the LORD lives and as you live, I will not leave you." So the two of them walked on.

Fifty men of the company of the prophets went and stood at a distance, facing the place where Elijah and Elisha had stopped at the Jordan. Elijah took his cloak, rolled it up and struck the water with it. The water divided to the right and to the left, and the two of them crossed over on dry ground.

When they had crossed, Elijah said to Elisha, "Tell me, what can I do for you before I am taken from you?"

"Let me inherit a double portion of your spirit," Elisha replied.

"You have asked a difficult thing," Elijah said, "yet if you see me when I am taken from you, it will be yours—otherwise not."

As they were walking along and talking together, suddenly a chariot of fire and horses of fire appeared and separated the two of them, and Elijah went up to heaven in a whirlwind. Elisha saw this and cried out, "My father! My father! The chariots and horsemen of Israel!" And Elisha saw him no more. Then he took hold of his own clothes and tore them apart.

He picked up the cloak that had fallen from Elijah and went back and stood on the bank of the Jordan. Then he took the cloak that had fallen from him and struck the water with it. "Where now is the LORD, the God of Elijah?" he asked. When he struck the water, it divided to the right and to the left, and he crossed over.

The company of the prophets from Jericho, who were watching, said, "The spirit of Elijah is resting on Elisha." And they went to meet him and bowed to the ground before him. "Look," they said, "we your servants have fifty able men. Let them go and look for your master. Perhaps the Spirit of the LORD has picked him up and set him down on some mountain or in some valley."

"No," Elisha replied, "do not send them."

But they persisted until he was too ashamed to refuse. So he said, "Send them." And they sent fifty men, who searched for three days but did not find him. When they returned to Elisha, who was staying in Jericho, he said to them, "Didn't I tell you not to go?"

In ancient Canaan, Baal was known as "the Rider of the Clouds." He was a warlike weather deity. The billowing dark clouds of a storm were viewed as the battle chariot in which Baal rode, thundering forth his voice and carrying lightning as his spear. We have already seen a number of ways in which the narratives about Elijah challenged the worship of Baal in the prophet's own day. Baal had no command over storm, rain, fire, or fertility, for those were the gifts of Yahweh, the God of Israel.

Instead of granting Baal the epithet "Rider of the

Clouds," the Old Testament insists that this title properly belongs to the Lord (Deut. 33:26; Pss. 68:4; 104:3; Isa. 19:1). The Lord God of Israel rides the heavens in his storm chariot at the head of the heavenly armies (Pss. 68:17; 104:3; Ezek. 1; Joel 2:5; Hab. 3:8; Zech. 6:1-2; 1 Chron. 28:18; 2 Kings 7:6). Yahweh's chariot is in the whirlwind (Isa. 66:15; Jer. 4:13). The glory cloud, that pillar of fire and smoke that attested to the presence of God, preceded Israel into battle. God and the armies of heaven fought on Israel's behalf from within the cloud at the Reed Sea (Ex. 15:4, 19).

When Elisha saw the whirlwind, the fire and horses, the symbolism was unmistakable (2 Kings 2:11-12). The warrior God, the captain of the armies of heaven, had come to retrieve his servant and catch him up into his war chariot. Elijah had fought the good fight, and now his commander would take him out of the fray and into his heavenly reward.

The New Testament notes many parallels between the life of Jesus and that of Elijah. Not the least of these is the account of Jesus' ascension into heaven.[1] Jesus, like Elijah, was received into the clouds (Acts 1:9), and angels reminded the disciples of what Jesus had already taught them, that "this same Jesus, who has been taken from you into heaven, will come back in the same way you have seen him go into heaven" (Acts 1:11). In ways at once both like and unlike Elijah, Jesus would come again. The Son of Man (Dan. 7:13-14) "will appear in the sky, and all the nations of the earth will mourn. They will see the Son of Man coming on the clouds of the sky, with power and great glory" (Matt. 24:30; cf. 26:64; Mark 13:26; 14:62; Luke 21:27).

Most often in religious art, the second coming of Jesus is portrayed with billowing, fluffy, white, friendly clouds. Regrettably, such portrayals miss the point. When Jesus returns in the clouds, he comes as the divine warrior in his storm chariot at the head of the armies of heaven. The clouds are dark, laden with flashes of fire and a ripping wind, for he comes to judge the earth, to avenge himself on his enemies, and to establish his kingdom. John the apostle wrote (Rev. 1:7),

> Look, he is coming with the clouds,
>   and every eye will see him,
> even those who pierced him;
>   and all the peoples of the earth will mourn
>   because of him.
>   So shall it be! Amen.

Because the prophets were the emissaries of the divine warrior who fought in Israel's behalf, they were often found on the battlefield or giving oracles to Israel's kings about the conduct of warfare. The extensive oracles against foreign nations that are found in a number of prophetic books are a kind of verbal holy war against Israel's enemies.

When the chariot carried Elijah away, Elisha cried out, "My father! My father! The chariots and horsemen of Israel!" (2 Kings 2:12). Most readers mentally paraphrase this to something like "Elijah, Elijah! Look, here come the chariots and horsemen of Israel!" Although this understanding of Elisha's cry is plausible in the context, it is probably not correct. The identical utterance was made in reference to Elisha when he was near death (13:14), but there was no chariot to take him away. In 2 Kings 13:14, "the chariots and horsemen of Israel" is an epithet used to describe the prophet himself, and this is probably the correct understanding also in 2 Kings 2:12. In the warfare of ancient Israel, to have the prophet was to have the army of God (2 Kings 3:14–19; 6:8–12, 17).

The church, too, is called to warfare. Jesus is not only the great and final prophet, but also the captain of the Lord's armies (Rev. 19:11–16). He has fought our battles for us. He is worth more to us than any number of chariots and horses (Ps. 20:7). Of course, our warfare is different from the battles fought by ancient Israel. Our weapons are spiritual—they are the sword of the Spirit and the word of God. Our weapons are often words, principles, and arguments directed toward demolishing every pretense that sets itself up against God (2 Cor. 10:4–5). We wear unique armor into our spiritual warfare (Eph. 6). The captain of the armies of heaven, our commander and Savior, Jesus, goes with us into the battle.[2]

In the New Testament, Matthew models the relationship between John the Baptist and Jesus so that it mirrors aspects of the relationship between Elijah and Elisha.[3] It was at the Jordan River that both John and Elijah anointed their successors. Jesus and Elisha would both enjoy the presence of God's Spirit ("a double portion") in a measure beyond that of their predecessors. Moses had divided the Sea, and Elijah had divided the Jordan. Elisha, as the successor of both Moses and Elijah, demonstrated that the same Spirit rested upon him when he, too, divided the waters (2 Kings 2:8, 14).

In ancient Canaan, the river and the sea were the rivals of Baal.[4] Prince Sea and Judge River were his enemies. They threatened to destroy him if he could not successfully overcome them. In the Old Testament, however, the sea and the river do not threaten Yahweh; rather, he rules over them, and they do his bidding (Gen. 1:2; Josh. 3:8; 4:18; Judg. 5:21; Ps. 46:4; Isa. 41:18; Dan. 7:10; cf. Rev. 22:1–2). Just as Elisha exercised dominion over the Jordan in the name of the Lord, the God of Elijah (2 Kings 2:14), so too Jesus would rule over the storm on the Sea of Galilee, the source of the Jordan (Luke 8:22–25). The wind and the waves would obey him.

The watery depths were often representative of death in the Old Testament (e.g., Jonah 2:3–6; Ps. 69:1–2). Elijah crossed through the depths of the Jordan and was received into the presence of God. We, too, face the depths unafraid and look forward to our own resurrection, to being "caught up . . . in the clouds to meet the Lord in the air. And so we will be with the Lord forever" (1 Thess. 4:17).

Elijah's mantle was a symbol of the way in which the Spirit of God had clothed him (see chapter 4, section B, "Elijah's Heir and Successor"). When Elisha struck the water with Elijah's mantle, the prophets at the river's edge knew immediately that "the spirit of Elijah is resting on Elisha" (2 Kings 2:15). John came dressed like Elijah (2 Kings 1:8; Matt. 3:4), and there at the Jordan anointed his successor. Instead of the river opening, it was the heavens that opened; God's Spirit descended on and enfolded Jesus (Matt. 3:16–17). Elisha had asked for a double portion of the Spirit that rested on Elijah. The "double portion" was the inheritance allotted to the firstborn son in Israel (Deut. 21:17). Similarly, when the Spirit descended upon Jesus, God's own voice testified from heaven, "'This is my beloved son,' here is my firstborn."

FOR FURTHER REFLECTION

1. Think of some of the ways in which the Bible reveals God as the divine warrior. How is this image applied to Jesus in the Scriptures?
2. Jesus has once for all defeated Satan, death, and the grave. Yet until he returns to banish evil and to reorder creation, we are to be engaged in spiritual warfare. In what ways are you aware of this battle? What are you doing to overcome evil in your own life and in this world?
3. Life is a battle. Where do you see conflict in your own life? How are you fighting it?

4. The prophet's mantle was a physical symbol of his having been clothed with the Spirit of God. The New Testament often makes use of similar clothing imagery in Romans 13:14; 1 Corinthians 15:53–54; 2 Corinthians 5:2; Ephesians 4:24; Colossians 3:10, 12; and 1 Peter 5:5. Think about these passages.
5. Was Elisha greedy in his desire for a "double portion"? Why or why not?

B. A TALE OF TWO CITIES
2 KINGS 2:19–25

The men of the city said to Elisha, "Look, our lord, this town is well situated, as you can see, but the water is bad and the land is unproductive."

"Bring me a new bowl," he said, "and put salt in it." So they brought it to him.

Then he went out to the spring and threw the salt into it, saying, "This is what the Lord says: 'I have healed this water. Never again will it cause death or make the land unproductive.'" And the water has remained wholesome to this day, according to the word Elisha had spoken.

From there Elisha went up to Bethel. As he was walking along the road, some youths came out of the town and jeered at him. "Go on up, you baldhead!" they said. "Go on up, you baldhead!" He turned around, looked at them and called down a curse on them in the name of the Lord. Then two bears came out of the woods and mauled forty-two of the youths. And he went on to Mount Carmel and from there returned to Samaria.

Jericho was an oasis located in the Jordan valley, a few miles north of the Dead Sea, at the mouth of the

Wadi Qilt. The Wadi Qilt formed a magnificent canyon descending from the hills west of the Jordan valley. At the valley floor, several springs erupted to provide the area with an abundant water supply. Today the warm temperatures and ample water make the region around Jericho productive for citrus trees and other crops.

Jericho had a checkered history, however. When Israel first entered the land and fought at Jericho, Joshua uttered a curse on the city: "Cursed before the LORD is the man who undertakes to rebuild this city, Jericho. At the cost of his firstborn son will he lay its foundations; at the cost of his youngest will he set up its gates" (Josh. 6:26). The story of the evils that existed in Israel during the reign of Ahab begins with the announcement that "in Ahab's time, Hiel of Bethel rebuilt Jericho. He laid its foundations at the cost of his firstborn son Abiram, and he set up its gates at the cost of his youngest son Segub, in accordance with the word of the LORD spoken by Joshua son of Nun" (1 Kings 16:34).

The short account in 2 Kings 2:19–22 is tantalizing in part because of what it does not tell us. No explanation is provided for how the spring had become poisoned, how long it had been so, or why salt was thrown into the water. Lacking some help in the text itself on these questions, it is probably better to avoid speculation.

What is clear from the text is that after Elisha's action, the water became wholesome and the land was restored to productivity. Keep in mind the nature of miracles in the Bible: (1) miracles are redemptive—they restore to pristine condition and rectify that which is wrong, and (2) because they restore to wholeness, miracles point toward the future and anticipate the new heavens and the new earth. In the healing of the waters at Jericho, we have a foretaste of the restoration of paradise and the removal of the curse to which creation was subjected through sin. It is not just people that are redeemed, but the creation itself. The creation was subjected to decay and frustration, and it longs for its own redemption (Rom. 8:20–22). At Jericho, a small piece of creation was relieved of its own corruption and decay; in this small demonstration of God's power, we look forward to the renewal of the heavens and the earth.

In describing the glorious future of a renewed creation, it is striking that Ezekiel includes in it the transformation of the Dead Sea just to the south of Jericho (Ezek. 47:1–12). Whereas Elisha added salt to the spring at Jericho, the salt of the Dead Sea would be removed by a life-giving river flowing from the presence of God. In both cases, creation is delivered from futility and barrenness. Our own lives are renewed by life-giving waters (John 4:10–14; 7:37–39), and creation shall be as well (Rev. 22:1–3).

In Israel in the ninth century B.C., Baal had claimed dominion over the rains and the waters. But once again, through story and event, God proclaimed that he ruled over the waters and that Baal was a delusion.

"TO KILL A MOCKING BOY"

At first glance, the story of the spring at Jericho and the story of the mocking boys at Bethel do not appear to be related. But there are connections. It was Hiel of Bethel who mocked God by fortifying a city that God had cursed (1 Kings 16:34). It was the citizens of Bethel who had mocked God with golden calves, idols that were proclaimed as the gods that had redeemed Israel from Egypt (12:28–29). The sons are like the fathers—it is not surprising to find mockers among the young men of Bethel.

The Scriptures depict mocking almost uniformly as the action of the ungodly (Ps. 1:1; Prov. 1:22; 13:1; 24:9; 29:8). In mocking, we ridicule those who have been made in the image of God, and therefore ridicule the God who made them. Perhaps James had these two stories (the healing of the spring at Jericho and the mocking boys) in mind when he wrote, "With the tongue we praise our Lord and Father, and with it we curse men, who have been made in God's likeness. . . . Can both fresh water and salt water flow from the same spring?" (James 3:9–11).

Mocking is among the most destructive things one person can do to another. More particularly, to mock God's messenger is to mock the One who has sent him.

Keep in mind once again the way in which miracles in the Bible point toward the end of time. These young men mocked Elisha, and God judged them for their mockery. What was true for the individual would also be true for the nation. Israel mocked her prophets (2 Chron. 36:16), and God judged his people in the destruction of Jerusalem. A great bear in the form of Nebuchadnezzar came from Babylon and mauled the nation. Israel's Messiah was also mocked, and in mocking the Son that God had sent, people were mocking the almighty God (Pss. 22:7; 89:50–51; Isa. 50:6; Matt. 20:19; 27:29, 31, 41). This mockery, too, would be avenged.

Paul articulated the principle quite clearly. He said, "Do not be deceived: God cannot be mocked. A man reaps what he sows" (Gal. 6:7). A harvest of what we have sown is coming (Gal. 6:9). On that day God will mock the mockers (Prov. 3:34), and he will have the last laugh.

Once again, some of the details of the text are not clear. Elijah was a hairy man (2 Kings 1:8), but Elisha was balding. The balding pate of the prophet appears to have provided a vehicle for ridicule that ultimately had little to do with baldness. The young men taunted, "Go on up, baldy!" "Go up" where? Were they telling him to leave town, to "go up" to the high place at Bethel, or to "go up" the way Elijah had done (2 Kings 2:11)? We cannot know. But it was enough that the prophet called down a curse on his tormentors.

It is striking that some of the mockery of Jesus was directed toward his head and included pulling out his hair (Isa. 50:6) and placing a crown of thorns on it. There is also a striking difference. When Jesus was mocked and tormented, the crowd bayed the opposite of Elisha's tormentors: "Come down!" they jeered (Matt. 27:40, 42). But in the midst of mocking, even by those who were crucified with him (Matt. 27:44), Jesus promised to take one to paradise with him (Luke 23:40–43) and prayed for the others, "Father, forgive them, for they do not know what they are doing" (Luke 23:34). Jesus opened a way so that sinful mockery could be forgiven.

FOR FURTHER REFLECTION

1. Miracles are redemptive and eschatological: they restore something that is awry to a pristine state, and they anticipate the renewal of the heavens and the earth. Think of other miracles in the Bible and how they show both of these characteristics.
2. How did the miracle that healed the waters strike a blow against Baal?
3. To mock God's prophet is to mock God, so closely is the word of God identified with the person of God. How is the word of God mocked today in our society? In our churches? In our own lives? The goal of the forgiveness that Christ offers to us is that we might be renewed and obey him. How do you need to change?
4. The Bible instructs us to do more than simply refrain from mocking God. What can we do positively to avoid mocking God?
5. In this chapter, we noted that human beings, made in the image of God, are often the recipients of our mocking. Whom do we mock and deride? Why are we so prone to mock others?

7

DÉJÀ VU

The next two stories should sound familiar to us. If we go back to 1 Kings 17:7–16, we read a story similar to 2 Kings 4:1–7. In both stories, the prophet miraculously supplies food in a time of great need. In the next story (2 Kings 4:8–37), we hear echoes from 1 Kings 17:17–24. In these stories, women who have supported the prophet lose a child, but God uses the prophet to bring the child back to life. The stories are not identical in detail, but they are similar in their main themes. The comparison demonstrates that God continues to work through Elisha, even though Elijah is now gone.

A. A PROPHET'S POOR WIDOW
2 KINGS 4:1–7

The wife of a man from the company of the prophets cried out to Elisha, "Your servant my husband is dead, and you know that he revered the LORD. But now his creditor is coming to take my two boys as his slaves."

Elisha replied to her, "How can I help you? Tell me, what do you have in your house?"

"Your servant has nothing there at all," she said, "except a little oil."

Elisha said, "Go around and ask all your neighbors for empty jars. Don't ask for just a few. Then go inside and shut the door behind you and your sons. Pour oil into all the jars, and as each is filled, put it to one side."

She left him and afterward shut the door behind her and her sons. They brought the jars to her and she kept pouring. When all the jars were full, she said to her son, "Bring me another one."

But he replied, "There is not a jar left." Then the oil stopped flowing.

She went and told the man of God, and he said, "Go, sell the oil and pay your debts. You and your sons can live on what is left."

There was no Social Security system in ancient Israel. God in his wisdom had provided laws and customs for Israel so that families were responsible to provide care during old age or indigence. Particularly the laws pertaining to the kinsman redeemer, the Jubilee and sabbatical years (Lev. 25:25–55), gleaning (Deut. 24:19–22), levirate marriage (Deut. 25:5–10; Ruth), and the strict regulation of lending practices (Ex. 22:25; Lev. 25:36–37; Deut. 23:19–20; Ps. 15:5; Ezek. 18:8) were designed to keep Israelite men and women out of debt bondage and within the care of a family unit (cf. 1 Tim. 5:3–4; James 1:27). God, who had redeemed Israel from slavery in Egypt, provided that his people would not fall into bondage again (Ex. 3:6; 6:6; 13:3, 14; Lev. 25:42; 26:13; Deut. 15:15; 24:18, 22).

Yet this text is silent about these provisions. Perhaps the widow had no relatives to redeem her property or children, and no family was willing to take her and her children into their household. For whatever reason, she and her children had dropped through the social safety net, and now her children were about to be enslaved to cover debts.

Things have not changed much between the Testaments, at least in one respect: God has "chosen those who are poor in the eyes of the world to be rich in faith and to inherit the kingdom he promised those who love him" (James 2:5). The poor widow's husband may or may not have provided effectively for his family—the text is silent about this, too. But he apparently had been a faithful (though anonymous) member of the band of prophets; he had "revered the LORD" (2 Kings 4:1). Although he had evidently not been rich as people would count wealth, he had been rich toward God and had treasure stored up in heaven (Luke 12:21). In the Old Testament, no less than in the New, God's promise stands: "Seek first his kingdom and his righteousness, and all these things will be given to you as well" (Matt. 6:33). Our heavenly father knows what we need.

Our weakness is always an opportunity for God to show his strength (1 Cor. 1:25, 27; 12:22; 2 Cor. 12:5–10; 13:4). The poor and the weak are the particular objects of his care. God himself "defends the cause of the fatherless and the widow, and loves the alien, giving him food and clothing" (Deut. 10:18; cf. Ex. 22:22; Deut. 14:29; Ps. 68:5; Isa. 1:17, 23; Jer. 22:3; Ezek. 22:7; Zech. 7:10; Mal. 3:5). Like the destitute widow and son to whom Elijah was sent at Zarephath (1 Kings 17:7–16), this widow found that her oil would flow until she had enough to pay her debts.

The debts they could not pay were paid by God. He was their Redeemer, and he is ours. The greatest debt we all have is the mortgage on our souls. It is a debt we cannot pay. But God can pay it. He has paid it by giving his own Son as a ransom for our souls. In a sense, this woman's sons were saved from debt bondage because God was their near kinsman and Redeemer; his own Son would pay their debts and ours.

The widow's sons were subject to bondage because they had been put up as a pledge or surety for an obligation, as a guarantee and collateral that the debt would be paid. God, too, has made a promise, and the surety of his obligation is his Son. "Jesus has become the guarantee of a better covenant" (Heb. 7:22).

Little is said about the creditor who threatened to take the widow's sons. Jesus would later tell a parable about a similar man who was forgiven an enormous debt that he could not repay, but then showed no mercy to someone who owed him a much smaller sum (Matt. 18:23–35). In this story, too, a monetary debt is used to illustrate a spiritual principle: When we owe so much to a forgiving God, we dare not withhold forgiveness from others (Matt. 18:35; cf. Mark 12:40; Luke 20:47).

Once again, keep in mind the nature of miracle in the Bible. Miracles are redemptive, and they point toward the future restoration of the cosmos. It is easy to see how this miraculous flow of oil was redemptive in sparing the widow's sons from bondage. It also points to the future in that it anticipates the renewal of the heavens and the earth. In paradise restored, there will be no want, hunger, pain, or fear. The Old Testament often portrays the blessedness of the eschatological future in terms of agricultural prosperity (Amos 9:13–15; Joel 3:18; Ezek. 47:12; Zech. 3:10). The widow and her sons enjoyed a foretaste of that plenty and their redemption.

FOR FURTHER REFLECTION

1. The prophet's widow experienced a crisis in her life. With no husband to turn to, she appealed to the prophet Elisha. When you face a crisis, to whom do you turn?

2. God finds opportunities in our weaknesses. Where are you weak? Do you see God's power in those areas of your life?

3. The multiplication of the oil reminds us of the multiplication of loaves and fishes many years later in Galilee. Whereas Elisha asked the widow, "What do you have in your house?" Jesus would later ask, "How many loaves do you have?" (Mark 6:38). Jesus was the prophet like Elisha, but even greater. In both cases, God multiplied what he had already given. How do you experience his provision for your needs?

4. Oil is often symbolic of the Holy Spirit. God is not miserly toward those who come to him in their need. He multiplied the widow's oil until her house could contain no more. When Jesus taught his disciples to pray, he encouraged them to ask, seek, and knock; he gave them this reassurance: "How much more will your Father in heaven give the Holy Spirit to those who ask him!" (Luke 11:9–13). Think about your prayer life. Does it need to change? If so, how?

5. What do people owe you? Are you an unforgiving creditor?

B. A FAMILY AT SHUNEM
2 KINGS 4:8–37

One day Elisha went to Shunem. And a well-to-do woman was there, who urged him to stay for a meal. So whenever he came by, he stopped there to eat. She said to her husband, "I know that this man who often comes our way is a holy man of God. Let's make a small room on the roof and put in it a bed and a table, a chair and a lamp for him. Then he can stay there whenever he comes to us."

One day when Elisha came, he went up to his room and lay down there. He said to his servant Gehazi, "Call the Shunammite." So he called her, and she stood before him. Elisha said to him, "Tell her, 'You have gone to all this trouble for us. Now what can be done for you? Can we speak on your behalf to the king or the commander of the army?'"

She replied, "I have a home among my own people."

"What can be done for her?" Elisha asked.

Gehazi said, "Well, she has no son and her husband is old."

Then Elisha said, "Call her." So he called her, and she stood in the doorway. "About this time next year," Elisha said, "you will hold a son in your arms."

"No, my lord," she objected. "Don't mislead your servant, O man of God!"

But the woman became pregnant, and the next year about that same time she gave birth to a son, just as Elisha had told her.

The child grew, and one day he went out to his father, who was with the reapers. "My head! My head!" he said to his father.

His father told a servant, "Carry him to his mother." After the servant had lifted him up and carried him to his mother, the boy sat on her lap until noon, and then he died. She went up and laid him on the bed of the man of God, then shut the door and went out.

She called her husband and said, "Please send me one of the servants and a donkey so I can go to the man of God quickly and return."

"Why go to him today?" he asked. "It's not the New Moon or the Sabbath."

"It's all right," she said.

She saddled the donkey and said to her servant, "Lead on; don't slow down for me unless I tell you." So she set out and came to the man of God at Mount Carmel.

When he saw her in the distance, the man of God said to his servant Gehazi, "Look! There's the Shunammite! Run to meet her and ask her, 'Are you all right? Is your husband all right? Is your child all right?'"

"Everything is all right," she said.

When she reached the man of God at the mountain, she took hold of his feet. Gehazi came over to push her away, but the man of God said, "Leave her alone! She is in bitter distress, but the LORD has hidden it from me and has not told me why."

"Did I ask you for a son, my lord?" she said. "Didn't I tell you, 'Don't raise my hopes'?"

Elisha said to Gehazi, "Tuck your cloak into your belt, take my staff in your hand and run. If you meet anyone, do not greet him, and if anyone greets you, do not answer. Lay my staff on the boy's face."

But the child's mother said, "As surely as the LORD lives and as you live, I will not leave you." So he got up and followed her.

Gehazi went on ahead and laid the staff on the boy's face, but there was no sound or response. So Gehazi went back to meet Elisha and told him, "The boy has not awakened."

When Elisha reached the house, there was the boy lying dead on his couch. He went in, shut the door on the two of them and prayed to the LORD. Then he got on the bed and lay upon the boy, mouth to mouth, eyes to eyes, hands to hands. As he stretched himself out upon him, the boy's body grew warm. Elisha turned away and walked back and forth in the room and then got on the bed and stretched out upon him once more. The boy sneezed seven times and opened his eyes.

Elisha summoned Gehazi and said, "Call the Shunammite." And he did. When she came, he said, "Take your son." She came in, fell at his feet and bowed to the ground. Then she took her son and went out.

This story contrasts with the preceding one in a number of respects. God's care is not confined to the poor, but also extends to those who are well-off. The woman in 2 Kings 4:1–7 was quite poor and yet had sons. The woman from Shunem, on the other hand, was well-to-do (v. 8). Instead of facing deprivation, as did the widow in the preceding account, she was able to house and feed the prophet on occasion. She had servants and livestock. She was secure and had "a home among my own people" (v. 13). She would probably never face a creditor or lack for care.[1] But she had no son.

It is difficult for modern Western readers to appreciate the depth of desire and the cultural pressure for a male heir in ancient Israel. Rights of inheritance ordinarily followed the male line, and the male lineage perpetuated the family name in Israel. The text does not indicate whether the woman and her husband had any daughters. The impression is left that the woman was barren, a condition that often caused grief (Gen. 11:30; 25:21; 29:31; Ex. 23:26; 1 Sam. 2:5; Job 24:21; Ps. 113:9; Prov. 30:16; Isa. 54:1; Luke 1:7, 36; 23:29; Gal. 4:27; Heb. 11:11). Her husband was old (2 Kings 4:14), but, as with Abraham and Sarah before them (Gen. 11:30) and Zechariah and Elizabeth after them (Luke 1:7, 36), God would grace their lives with a promised child.

Jesus later enunciated the principle: "He who receives you receives me, and he who receives me receives the one who sent me. Anyone who receives a prophet because he is a prophet will receive a prophet's reward" (Matt. 10:40–41). The woman's selfless provision for God's servant would not go unrewarded.

Shunem was about twenty miles from Mount Carmel, and on one occasion when the prophet stopped at the woman's home, he asked if there was any service he could render to her. Her response was one of contentment with her life (2 Kings 4:13), perhaps fearing that to ask for a son would be more than could be expected, or simply graciously declining the prophet's offer to intervene with the governmental authorities.

Like the faith of the gentile widow to whom Elijah ministered (1 Kings 17), this woman's faith was expressed (2 Kings 4:8–17), tested (4:18–28), and ratified (4:29–37) through these events. Her initial joy gave way to dismay and confusion, only to be restored with the restoration of the child.

There is much to be learned about faith in the woman's actions. When her child fell ill, she proceeded with haste and dogged determination to reach the prophet. There was no wavering on her part. She did not inform her husband that the child had died; she assured her husband and Gehazi that all was or would be well if only she could find Elisha.

Faith is continuing to believe in the promises and goodness of God. Faith is considering it certain that God will be true to his word. It is knowing that he is able to do immeasurably more than all we ask or imagine (Eph. 3:20). God does not mislead or deceive us (2 Kings 4:16, 28).

What was required for the boy to be revived?

First, the prophet sent his staff ahead in the hands of his servant Gehazi. Gehazi's errand was urgent, and he was to place the prophet's staff on the boy's face. It is probably not possible for us to know with confidence what this gesture represented. Perhaps the prophet likened his staff to Moses' rod in the wilderness (Ex. 4:2, 4, 17; 7:17–20; 8:5–17; 9:23; 14:16; 17:9; Num. 20:7–11). The staff may have been emblematic of the prophet and his office, a visible token that he was on his way (Gen. 38:18, 25; 49:10; Num. 17:1–10). It could have been emblematic of God's own staff as the Shepherd of Israel, the staff that comforted in the valley of the shadow of death (Ps. 23:4). Whatever symbolism may have been involved with the staff, it garnered no response.

Second, once the prophet arrived, he and the boy's mother prayed in the child's behalf (2 Kings 4:33). But, once again, there was no response.

Finally, much as Elijah had done with the widow's son (1 Kings 17:21), Elisha stretched himself out over the boy's body, matching joint to joint, mouth to mouth, eye to eye, and hand to hand (2 Kings 4:34). In this way the prophet identified himself with the boy in his mortality and death, and only then was life restored to the child (v. 35).

Christians cannot read this story without thinking of an even greater successor to Elisha. Two faithful women, Mary and Martha, sought Jesus when their brother Lazarus died. Jesus, too, was delayed in his arriving at the home of the deceased (John 11:6). There Jesus taught Mary and Martha that he was the resurrection and the life, and that those who believe in him would not die (vv. 25–26). At Lazarus's tomb, those who believed, like this Shunammite woman of old, saw the glory of God (v. 40).

Shunem was located on the southwestern slope of the hill of Moreh along the edge of the plain of Jezreel. Just a couple miles away was the site where the village of Nain would be located in the New Testament period. It was to this tiny village that one greater than both Elijah and Elisha came. There he encountered the funeral procession for the only son of a local widow, and Jesus restored the child's life by his command. The crowd was correct in their response, "A great prophet has appeared among us. God has come to help his people" (Luke 7:16).

Like all miracles, the miracle Elisha performed for the Shunammite widow's son pointed to the future. It anticipated and provided a foretaste of the resurrection of the dead. But it also did more than that. It showed in some measure how God would accomplish this resurrection. He would send his own Son to identify with us and to take on our humanity and mortality (Phil. 2:5–11; Heb. 2:14–15). We are raised to life because of his resurrection; our lives are hidden with Christ in God (Col. 3:1–3).

FOR FURTHER REFLECTION

1. In the previous story, God used the prophet to minister to a poor woman. In the present story, God, through the prophet, aided a rich woman. God is not a respecter of persons. Do you love all people equally, or do you favor the poor (or the rich)?

2. The wealthy woman at Shunem seemed to lack nothing. Although she dared not ask for a son (perhaps in light of so many unanswered prayers before this time), her response to Elisha's announcement reveals the depth of her desire and her fear of disappointment. The Lord knows our needs, even when we are reluctant to admit them. How do you find contentment when a deep desire of the heart remains unfulfilled?

3. The woman's son died, but her faith in the Lord did not die. Her faith persisted and asserted itself even in the face of death. Her hopes and expectations for this promised child compelled her to believe that God would not abandon the child to death. The son given to the Virgin Mary also died

in spite of the hopes and expectations of many. They had expected a king, and then they had a crucified corpse. How often in the Bible God's greater plans are revealed when he shatters the expectations of his people! Have you seen God grant your hopes and desires, only to watch them wither and die? Have you been able to see his better plan for your life?

4. What do you make of Gehazi's failure? Of Elisha's success?

5. The son of the Shunammite woman would eventually die, just as Lazarus did. Although these "temporary resurrections" pointed forward to God's power over death and the grave, only Jesus would rise from the grave never to die again. He said, "Because I live, you also will live" (John 14:19). How do the hopes of eternal life change your perspective on the hopes, desires, and expectations of this life?

8

MORE MIRACLES

G od used the prophets to bring his message of judgment and repentance to the people. To attest to their divine appointment, God worked miracles through them. The following two sections record some of the most striking wonders in the Old Testament.

A. TWO MEALS
2 KINGS 4:38–44

Elisha returned to Gilgal and there was a famine in that region. While the company of the prophets was meeting with him, he said to his servant, "Put on the large pot and cook some stew for these men."

One of them went out into the fields to gather herbs and found a wild vine. He gathered some of its gourds and filled the fold of his cloak. When he returned, he cut them up into the pot of stew, though no one knew what they were. The stew was poured out for the men, but as they began to eat it, they cried out, "O man of God, there is death in the pot!" And they could not eat it.

Elisha said, "Get some flour." He put it into the pot and said, "Serve it to the people to eat." And there was nothing harmful in the pot.

A man came from Baal Shalishah, bringing the man of God twenty loaves of barley bread baked from the first ripe grain, along with some heads of new grain. "Give it to the people to eat," Elisha said.

"How can I set this before a hundred men?" his servant asked.

But Elisha answered, "Give it to the people to eat. For this is what the LORD says: 'They will eat and have some left over.'" Then he set it before them, and they ate and had some left over, according to the word of the LORD.

It is striking how many of the stories about Elijah and Elisha have to do with food. It is difficult for modern Western readers to understand what life in an agrarian society at basically subsistence levels meant for the average individual in ancient Israel. Starvation and hard times were never far away. Disruption of the annual rainy season, molds and funguses from too much or too little rain, locust outbreaks, or raiders who confiscated the harvest for their own use or burned the fields in order to force the population to surrender could rapidly reduce an already hard life to a borderline existence. News photos of famine-ravaged countries in our own day dramatically show how precarious life can be in agrarian societies. In modern Western countries, food is a far smaller part of a household budget than it has ever been; the time invested in gathering it is ordinarily limited to how long one spends in a supermarket or convenience store and perhaps a small family garden. Life was very different in ancient Israel. In subsistence or marginal economies, providing daily bread may represent the largest expenditure one makes and may also consume almost every waking moment.

Many read some of the stories about Elisha and come to the opinion that they trivialize miracles. As in the case of the floating axhead or the mauling bears, the end achieved by this miracle—making the pottage edible (2 Kings 4:38–41)—seems somehow less worthwhile or impressive than other miracles, where life and health are restored. God's power is reduced to the semimagical removal of an inconvenience rather than the removal of a formidable or impossible obstacle like death or leprosy. After all, how long would it take to make another pot of soup!

Such a reading of the story misses the point, however. A famine was abroad in the region around Gilgal (2 Kings 4:38). When Elisha arrived, he saw that the community of prophets was in need of food. The scarcity of food was demonstrated when one of the men went out into the surrounding fields to gather edible herbs. While he was searching for edible plants, he found a wild vine with what appeared to be an edible fruit or gourd. There is a wild vine that grows in Israel with fruit about the size and shape of an orange; its taste is extremely bitter. Other passages mention poisonous or noxious flora in the land (Deut. 29:18; 32:32; Hos. 10:4). The man scavenging for food did not recognize the potentially toxic effects of what he had gathered.

God had already used Elijah and Elisha to provide for starving widows and their families (1 Kings 17:7–16; 2 Kings 4:1–7), and he would not do less for his hungry servants. This miracle not only redeemed the pottage, but also redeemed the labor of those who had prepared it.

All of our labor in this world is tainted with flaws, inadequacy, failure, and sinfulness. Imagine what the scavenging prophet was thinking: "I should have stayed in bed. Nothing I do goes right. Now the whole group is upset with me! What's the point in trying?" Some people are what one pastor-friend of mine called "emotional black holes": no matter how many hundreds of hours and thousands of dollars are poured into trying to help them, at the end you find yourself only discouraged and exhausted, with no perceptible change in them. On other occasions, when you thought you were doing right by a child or family member, you find out instead that you have hurt someone you love. The writer of Ecclesiastes recognized so clearly how futile and pointless human effort can be.

What do we learn about God from this short account? We see that his power and provision extend to what may be the lesser and more mundane moments of life. We see a miracle that anticipates the restoration and perfection of creation. In a new heaven and a new earth, the thorns, thistles, and poisons that frustrate our labor will be gone (Gen. 3:18). But perhaps most pointedly, we see our God redeeming the labor of his servants, so that it would not be done in vain. Paul would later express this quite clearly. At the end of an extended discussion of the redemption accomplished by Christ in his resurrection, he says, "Always give yourselves fully to the work of the Lord, because you know that your labor in the Lord is not in vain" (1 Cor. 15:58). The significance of the resurrection is not just out there in the future somewhere, but rather is far more immediate and tangible. The efforts of the men to provide a meal were not in vain; the giving of a cup of cold water will not be in vain (Matt. 10:42), nor will the rest of our labor. In the face of the frailty, transitoriness, and futility of human life, God in Christ would answer Moses' prayer: "[Lord,] establish the work of our hands" (Ps. 90:17).

Presumably the famine was continuing when the man from Baal Shalisha brought the community of prophets twenty loaves of bread and some grain from his freshly harvested fields (2 Kings 4:42–44). The famine was probably at its peak just before the harvest, and the man's offering to the prophets speaks loudly of his giving to God from the first and best that he had, even in adverse conditions.

It was a generous gift, even if it was scarcely enough to feed all those who were there. But Elisha's command to "give it to the people to eat" was accompanied by God's own provision, so that the word of the Lord was fulfilled, "They will eat and have some left over."

God had earlier shown his concern for the people's hunger during their years in the wilderness. He fed the nation with bread from heaven, manna, so that they would not be hungry in that desolate land. Once again, a miracle of feeding anticipates the restoration of paradise; it points to God's bounteous garden, paradise restored, where there will be no hunger or want.

Eight centuries later, Jesus was surrounded by his disciples and a large, hungry crowd (Matt. 14:13–21; Mark 6:32–44; Luke 9:10–17; John 6:5–13). The disciples estimated that to feed them would require a sum equivalent to eight months of a man's wages (Mark 6:37). Instead of the twenty loaves that Elisha had, there were five loaves and two fishes. But five thousand men ate, and there was food to spare (Mark 6:42–44; cf. 2 Kings 4:44). Later Jesus would repeat this miracle for a crowd of four thousand (Matt. 15:32–39; Mark 8:1–10).

When Jesus fed the five thousand, the crowd knew that a prophet was in their midst (John 6:14). They had been anticipating the coming of the prophet who would be like Moses (Deut. 18:15, 18), one who would do the signs and wonders that Moses had done (Deut. 34:10–12). Jesus fed the people in a remote place, just as Moses had fed them in the wilderness. Elisha had also fed a large crowd from a small amount of food. But now one greater than Moses and greater than Elisha had come.

Moses and Elisha had satisfied the people's physical hunger for a time. But after Jesus fed the five thousand and crossed the Sea of Galilee, he spoke to them of more than physical hunger. He proclaimed himself to be the bread that had come down from heaven, a food that would endure to eternal life (John 6:27). Those who come to him will never go hungry (John 6:35).

FOR FURTHER REFLECTION

1. We often take the basic necessities of life for granted, including food. The Elijah and Elisha stories often concern food and show us that it ultimately comes from the hand of God. Do you take the basic necessities of life for granted?

2. Have you experienced instances in your life where your best efforts were frustrated and a relationship or situation went from bad to worse? In retrospect, can you see how God has redeemed the situation?

3. Do you know any people whom you would categorize as "emotional back holes"? How would you characterize yourself with them? Your ministry to them?

4. Paul admonishes us, "Whatever you do, work at it with all your heart, as working for the Lord, not for men" (Col. 3:23). Almost all jobs, careers, and vocations are avenues to bring glory to God and to serve him. Have you ever committed your work to the service of the Lord? Do it now.

5. Our checkbooks show our true priorities. The man from Baal Shalishah brought the best of his harvest even during a famine. It is tempting to give God less than our first and best. We have so many bills and so little cash! Are you giving God your firstfruits?

B. A BATH FOR NAAMAN
2 KINGS 5

Now Naaman was commander of the army of the king of Aram. He was a great man in the sight of his master and highly regarded, because through him the LORD had given victory to Aram. He was a valiant soldier, but he had leprosy.

Now bands from Aram had gone out and had taken captive a young girl from Israel, and she served Naaman's wife. She said to her mistress, "If only my master would see the prophet who is in Samaria! He would cure him of his leprosy."

Naaman went to his master and told him what the girl from Israel had said. "By all means, go," the king of Aram replied. "I will send a letter to the king of Israel." So Naaman left, taking with him ten talents of silver, six thousand shekels of gold and ten sets of clothing. The letter that he took to the king of Israel read: "With this letter I am sending my servant Naaman to you so that you may cure him of his leprosy."

As soon as the king of Israel read the letter, he tore his robes and said, "Am I God? Can I kill and bring back to life? Why does this fellow send someone to me to be cured of his leprosy? See how he is trying to pick a quarrel with me!"

When Elisha the man of God heard that the king of Israel had torn his robes, he sent him this message: "Why have you torn your robes? Have the man come to me and he will know that there is a prophet in Israel." So Naaman went with his horses and chariots and stopped at the door of Elisha's house. Elisha sent a messenger to say to him, "Go, wash yourself seven times in the Jordan, and your flesh will be restored and you will be cleansed."

But Naaman went away angry and said, "I thought that he would surely come out to me and stand and call on the name of the LORD his God, wave his hand over the spot and cure me of my leprosy. Are not Abana and Pharpar, the rivers of Damascus, better than any of the waters of Israel?

Couldn't I wash in them and be cleansed?" So he turned and went off in a rage.

Naaman's servants went to him and said, "My father, if the prophet had told you to do some great thing, would you not have done it? How much more, then, when he tells you, 'Wash and be cleansed'!" So he went down and dipped himself in the Jordan seven times, as the man of God had told him, and his flesh was restored and became clean like that of a young boy.

Then Naaman and all his attendants went back to the man of God. He stood before him and said, "Now I know that there is no God in all the world except in Israel. Please accept now a gift from your servant."

The prophet answered, "As surely as the LORD lives, whom I serve, I will not accept a thing." And even though Naaman urged him, he refused.

"If you will not," said Naaman, "please let me, your servant, be given as much earth as a pair of mules can carry, for your servant will never again make burnt offerings and sacrifices to any other god but the LORD. But may the LORD forgive your servant for this one thing: When my master enters the temple of Rimmon to bow down and he is leaning on my arm and I bow there also—when I bow down in the temple of Rimmon, may the LORD forgive your servant for this."

"Go in peace," Elisha said.

After Naaman had traveled some distance, Gehazi, the servant of Elisha the man of God, said to himself, "My master was too easy on Naaman, this Aramean, by not accepting from him what he brought. As surely as the LORD lives, I will run after him and get something from him."

So Gehazi hurried after Naaman. When Naaman saw him running toward him, he got down from the chariot to meet him. "Is everything all right?" he asked.

"Everything is all right," Gehazi answered. "My master sent me to say, 'Two young men from the company of the prophets have just come to me from the hill country of Ephraim. Please give them a talent of silver and two sets of clothing.'"

"By all means, take two talents," said Naaman. He urged Gehazi to accept them, and then tied up the two talents of silver in two bags, with two sets of clothing. He gave them to two of his servants, and they carried them ahead of Gehazi. When Gehazi came to the hill, he took the things from the servants and put them away in the house. He sent the men away and they left. Then he went in and stood before his master Elisha.

"Where have you been, Gehazi?" Elisha asked.

"Your servant didn't go anywhere," Gehazi answered.

But Elisha said to him, "Was not my spirit with you when the man got down from his chariot to meet you? Is this the time to take money, or to accept clothes, olive groves, vineyards, flocks, herds, or menservants and maidservants? Naaman's leprosy will cling to you and to your descendants forever." Then Gehazi went from Elisha's presence and he was leprous, as white as snow.

This story is a study in contrasts: the wisdom of God versus the wisdom of human beings. God so often chooses insignificant means to accomplish his purposes. We have already seen in the Elijah and Elisha stories that the love of God is set particularly on the poor, the defenseless, the widow, and the orphan. Here God chooses an Israelite slave girl (2 Kings 5:2–3). There was little to commend her in the eyes of her Aramean master and mistress. She had probably been taken from Israel as part of the booty from an Aramean raid; she was living testimony to the effectiveness of Naaman as a military commander. She was an alien in a foreign land, without the rights enjoyed by those who were native-born. She was young, she was a woman, and she was a slave. One could scarcely find a person lower in the sociological hierarchy of ancient Aram.

Yet she was a woman who held steadfastly to her faith in Israel's God. She had learned what Peter would centuries later advise the infant church: "Always be prepared to give an answer to everyone who asks you to give the reason for the hope that you have" (1 Peter 3:15). A seed had been sown, and in time it would bear fruit a hundredfold.

If God would allow us to scan the book of life, whose names would we find there? Many would be recorded there who came to faith because of the influence of famous preachers or prominent celebrities. But I suspect that a far, far greater number would be there because of the faithful witness and hope-filled confidence of the humble people of this world.

The king of Aram was ready to make Naaman's leprosy[1] the occasion for an incident in his "cold war" with Israel—at least that is how the king of Israel perceived it (2 Kings 5:4–7). Naaman was ready to go to enormous expense. A shekel weighed about four-tenths of an ounce, and a talent weighed 70 to 75 pounds. This means that Naaman was bringing about 700 pounds of silver and 125 pounds of gold (v. 5). The ten sets of clothing were not "off the rack" from a retail store. Instead, they had no doubt been made from the finest materials, with emblems and decorations of gold and silver woven into and sewn on the garments; they were the kinds of garments that clothed idols, kings, and generals. The garments alone probably could have been a king's ransom.

But who would believe it? God's grace for Naaman was not going to cost him a cent. Grace is unmerited favor. By definition, it cannot be bought or earned, for then it would no longer be unmerited. God's grace was given freely to whomsoever he wished. God has no need of gold and silver; they cannot sway their Creator.

It has always been that way, for this is part of the character of God that remains the same in both Testaments. Salvation for Naaman, and for us, is through the free grace of God. Paul would later say that "it is by grace you have been saved, through faith—and this not from yourselves, it is the gift of God—not by works, so that no one can boast" (Eph. 2:8–9).

Many have found God's reaction to Gehazi's actions harsh. After Naaman left, Gehazi slipped away and caught up with the Aramean's entourage in order to obtain wealth for himself. Gehazi was disconcerted that God's grace had been shown to "this Aramean" (2 Kings 5:20). The translators of the New English Bible caught the gist quite well when Gehazi reacts, "What? Has my master let this Aramean go scot-free?" (v. 20). Gehazi would personally take plunder from an enemy. But instead of the riches he sought, Gehazi and his descendants got the leprosy that had adhered to Naaman (vv. 20–27). Why did God respond so harshly to the prophet's servant? In part, I suspect, it was because Gehazi was undoing what God had done: God wanted Naaman to know his free grace, but Gehazi was trying to put a price on the goodness of God. The God of Israel did not accept bribes; he would not be manipulated by money or make room for human pride. His grace was free. Gehazi was implying otherwise, and it would be at great cost to him. Our God can be as gracious to our enemies as he has been to us.

Elisha's encounter with Naaman is scarcely a model of "how to win friends and influence people." The commander of a foreign army showed up at the prophet's home, and the prophet would not so much as come out to greet him, sending out an intermediary instead (2 Kings 5:9–10). This was not conduct calculated to win a friend. Why did the prophet act that way? There were at least two reasons for it.

In the first place, the prophet was probably reacting to Naaman's expectation. Naaman expected Israel's God and prophet to be just like what he had known at home: itching palms and magic shows. He had brought plenty of money, and so he expected the prophet to deliver on the magic. Naaman wanted "vending machine grace"— put your money in and take your blessing. The prophet was expected to appear, accept the pay, and "wave his hand over the spot and cure me of my leprosy" (2 Kings 5:11).

Human beings have always wanted God to be subject to magic—how convenient it would be for us if we could coerce the deity by having the right magical formula! But the God of Israel does not give his sovereignty and glory to another. There would be no mumbo-jumbo here. God's prophet was not just a better magician than what Naaman had seen at home. Instead, the focus would be exclusively on the actions and grace of God. The prophet would allow no confusion: God, not the prophet's magic, would heal Naaman. To prevent the sort of confusion that Naaman's expectations would create, the prophet did not so much as meet the man when he first came to his door.

The second important factor that was operative here is perhaps less immediately clear from the text. Naaman was the commander of an enemy army. He had been effective in his missions against Israel, as the presence of an Israelite slave girl in his home suggests. The Arameans had been long-standing enemies, and they would come again to put Israel in dire straits (2 Kings 6:24–29; 13:4–7). Naaman was not a man for whom the average Israelite would wish health and long life—quite the contrary. Imagine how the average Kuwaiti felt about Iraq's Saddam Hussein during the 1991 Gulf War—that's probably close to how the Israelites felt about Naaman.

Yet in this incident we learn afresh something of the nature of God. He commands us to love our enemies, because in loving our enemies we are imitating him (Matt. 5:43–45; Luke 6:27, 35).

God had long ago appointed Israel to be a light to the nations. He had told Abraham that all the nations of the earth would be blessed through his descendants (Gen. 12:3; 18:18; 22:18). In Elisha's encounter with Naaman, we see the grace of God extended to the Gentiles, even to Israel's enemy. That must have been hard for Elisha. It was not a popular message to the Jews of Jesus' day either. After Jesus had been traveling through Galilee of the Gentiles and performing miracles there, he returned to his hometown of Nazareth and went to the synagogue. The people wanted him to do the same miracles for them that he had done for the Gentiles. Jesus explained his actions by saying, "There were many in Israel with leprosy in the time of Elisha the prophet, yet not one of them was cleansed—only Naaman the Syrian" (Luke 4:27). When they heard that, the crowd sought to take Jesus' life (vv. 28–30). "Don't tell us that God's grace is also for our enemies."

It is no surprise that Naaman did not want to get into the Jordan—not even once, much less seven times. It was not a very attractive river by comparison with the rushing, tumbling, cold waters of the Abana and Pharpar (2 Kings 5:12), rivers in Aram that formed from the melting snows of Mount Hermon. By comparison, the Jordan was tepid and lethargic through most of the year.

But Naaman's rage (v. 12) was not really about the choice of rivers. Naaman was simply not ready to humble himself. After all, anybody can wash in a river. For a man like Naaman, a more suitable challenge was necessary. Even Naaman's attendants could see the real issue (v. 13). If Elisha had said, "Go home and raise twice the money," that would have been a fitting demand for a man of his stature. After accomplishing such a task, Naaman would be able to boast that he had earned his healing.

The problem here is that the God who offers his grace freely also hates pride. To experience his grace, we must humble ourselves, realize our own inabilities, and look to him in our weakness, that we might see his strength. God is no respecter of persons: whether you are a Syrian general, a wealthy American, or the poorest peasant or leper, to know the grace of God, we must abandon our pride and pretension. It is God who saves—not we ourselves.

"Wash in the Jordan and be cured of leprosy." What a preposterous idea! I can't think of anything more ridiculous!

Well, maybe one thing is more ridiculous—the idea that putting your trust and faith in a man executed on a cross almost two thousand years ago can give you a renewed life now, forgiveness from sin, resurrection from the dead, and eternal life. Now that beats all!

God's promises always require faith. They always look foolish, improbable, unbelievable, unlikely, impossible. But God's seemingly foolish commands, when they are believed and obeyed, become the power of God—for Naaman and for us.

Water in the Bible is often symbolic of death (Jonah 2:3–5; Ps. 69:1–2). In a sense, Naaman's dips in the Jordan were death to his old life and a regeneration, a new birth in a new life (2 Kings 5:14).

Paul was a rabbi, steeped in the Hebrew Scriptures. I have always wondered if he did not have 2 Kings 5 in the back of his mind as he wrote 1 Corinthians 1:18–31.

Paul urged the early church, "Think of what you were when you were called. Not many of you were wise by human standards; not many were influential; not many were of noble birth" (1 Cor. 1:26). God chooses the lowly and despised, the foolish and weak things of this world, to nullify the boasting of the world (vv. 27–29). God chose a slave girl. He has chosen you and me.

Human beings consider the message of God's free grace, the message of the cross, foolishness—but for those of us who are being saved, it is the power of God (v. 18). God's foolishness is wiser than human wisdom!

If we are going to boast, let's boast in the Lord (v. 31). Boast of his wisdom, his power, his grace, his goodness, and his mercy.

FOR FURTHER REFLECTION

1. How do you suppose Naaman felt about God's wisdom while he had his leprosy? After he was healed and his pride had been humbled? It is often hard to see God's wisdom—what he is doing, how he is shaping us—in the middle of adversity. It's easier to see that in retrospect. Can you think of how this is true in your own life or the lives of others?

2. We admire the courage and faith of this Israelite slave girl. Even in what was an impossible situation, she still held tightly to her confidence in the God of Israel. Pray for similar courage and confidence; pray that you will be unashamed of the gospel.

3. In almost all religions, people must work their way to divine favor or earn their place in some

heaven. Why is this so appealing to so many people? Why is the cross such an offense to such beliefs?

4. What do you make of Naaman's request to continue to participate in the worship of Rimmon? Of the prophet's permission? Are there any modern analogies?

5. How have you seen God's use of the foolish and weak to shame the wise? In what instances have you observed it?

9

GOD IN THE LITTLE AND
THE BIG THINGS

The next two stories remind us that God is with us in all aspects of our life, from the smallest to the largest. The first story, about a floating axhead, illustrates how God works in our ordinary activities. The second narrates a life-and-death situation for the prophet and his company. Both stories not only comfort us in whatever distress overwhelms us, but also reveal to us a caring and powerful God.

A. THE FLOATING AXHEAD
2 KINGS 6:1–7

The company of the prophets said to Elisha, "Look, the place where we meet with you is too small for us. Let us go to the Jordan, where each of us can get a pole; and let us build a place there for us to live."

And he said, "Go."

Then one of them said, "Won't you please come with your servants?"

"I will," Elisha replied. And he went with them.

They went to the Jordan and began to cut down trees. As one of them was cutting down a tree, the iron axhead fell into the water. "Oh, my lord," he cried out, "it was borrowed!"

The man of God asked, "Where did it fall?" When he showed him the place, Elisha cut a stick and threw it there, and made the iron float. "Lift it out," he said. Then the man reached out his hand and took it.

There are several different approaches that we can take when reading a biblical text; each change of vantage point puts the passage in a different light. The account of Elisha's miraculous retrieval of an axhead is a good illustration.

Ordinarily when Christians pick up their Bibles and read a passage, especially when it's a story, the first question that comes to mind is something like, "What should I learn from this? How does it apply to me? What is here that I should emulate or avoid? How should my life change because of what I am reading?" These are good questions. They demonstrate a wholesome concern to be good disciples. We identify with the characters we are reading about. We see in their temptations and struggles the contours of our own daily struggle with sin; their successes and failures speak to us about analogous situations in our own lives and the lives of others.

When the story of the broken ax is approached this way, various biblical principles and admonitions come to mind. The Bible reminds us that "the borrower is servant to the lender" (Prov. 22:7) and warns us about the dangers of debt; we should "owe no man any thing" (Rom. 13:8 KJV). In a debt-ridden society such as our own, this is a timely and important observation.

I have asked other people what principles they see in this passage that bear on our conduct. Some have suggested the need for leaders to emulate the concern and compassion of Elisha for his workers. Others have mentioned the need to keep your tools in good shape and to be prepared for work. Others have seen a warning to be sure you have competent help: if you use volunteers, you too often get what you paid for. One man humorously suggested that the passage meant "Don't build on waterfront property."

All of these observations are interesting enough. A couple are perhaps more apt and useful. The Bible does urge us to imitate the actions of some and to avoid the folly of others (Deut. 18:9; 2 Kings 17:15; Ezek. 23:48; 1 Cor. 4:16; Eph. 5:1; 1 Thess. 1:6; 2:14; Heb. 6:12; 13:7; 3 John 11). But we can read other stories—for example, Aesop's fables or a Hemingway novel—the same way. We can identify with the characters in those stories and learn from them, too.

Is this what the Bible is teaching us from the passage? Was this why the passage was written? Most of us recognize that the answer is probably no. Useful principles are illustrated here, but the fact that a story illustrates some principle does not mean that it was written for that purpose. For that matter, all of life teaches us about wisdom and folly. We see wisdom and folly illustrated in our offices, relationships, the newspaper, books we read, and television we watch. But the book of Kings is not itself a collection of parables or wisdom literature, and we should not treat it as if it were. Can we do better?

The sorts of questions we ask of a text often determine the results. For example, all the questions in the preceding paragraphs are immediately concerned with application to individual lives. They all take anthropocentric approaches to the texts, centering on people and their needs.

Perhaps we should ask whether this is in keeping with the fundamental purpose of Scripture. We do want to learn how we should live when we read the Bible, but isn't the Bible more fundamentally a revelation about

God? That is, the Bible is concerned to make God known. It is his word to us about who he is and what he has done; we read it to learn about him. Rather than taking a predominantly anthropocentric approach to the Bible, we need to follow a more theocentric approach. If we do that, our first question will not be "What's here for me?" but rather "What do I learn about God from this passage?" Very different information comes into the spotlight with this question than with the former one. We see that God brings good out of evil, that he cares for his servants, that he rules over the laws of nature, that he is strong where we are weak, that his power accompanies his word, that he is concerned not only with the events of nations and important peoples, but also with the lesser details of the lives of little people. With this approach to the text, the focus shifts away from me and what I should or should not do. It goes instead to praise, adoration, thanks, and reverence toward God because of his power, goodness, and grace. God reveals what he is like in this story, and his attributes are the same as he deals with us. It fills us with wonder and awe as we think about him.

Remember that the ancient Canaanites viewed Judge River and Prince Sea as rivals of Baal who threatened to overwhelm and destroy him.[1] But here God shows again that the waters do not threaten him—rather, they do his bidding. The cosmos cannot be a rival to God, for he has created it and he rules over it to do his own good will. This miracle anticipates a future day when God will redeem the creation. In that day, the creation will no longer frustrate our labor as it has done since Adam's fall in the garden (Gen. 3:17–19); the creation will join in our labor instead of resisting it.

After learning from the passage more about what God is like, I can then ask, "How should I respond to this God?" The answers at least include confidence and joy that the same God watches over and cares for me. If he won't let a prophet lose an axhead, he certainly won't lose me when I've put my confidence in him (John 6:39; 2 Tim. 1:12).

For Christian readers of the Old Testament, there is yet another step to take. We have come to know God through Jesus Christ. How is what we learn of God in Christ related to what we learn of God from the Old Testament? Jesus is the same yesterday, today, and forever (Heb. 13:8). We need to ask, How can we see God in Christ reconciling the world to himself in the pages of the Hebrew Scriptures? That is, in addition to anthropocentric and theocentric ways of reading the Bible, there is also a Christocentric approach.

It is hard for us today to get upset if someone loses or breaks an ax or a pick borrowed from us. Such a tool is not terribly expensive, and if the borrower cannot replace it, for most of us it would not "break the bank" to purchase another one. However, in this regard we are worlds away from Israel in the ninth century B.C. We usually date the beginning of the Iron Age to around 1200 B.C. We know that for at least a time Israel lagged behind her neighbors in developing the technology to exploit this metal (1 Sam. 13:20–21). Iron implements would have been tremendously expensive. Many hours of labor would have been required to gather the wood for fires, to refine the ore, and then to shape and sharpen the tool. There was not much "discretionary income" in ancient Israel. Losing a borrowed axhead then would be comparable to wrecking a borrowed car today.

The young prophet seemed alarmed, probably because he recognized the tremendous debt facing him. How could he pay for an axhead? He was a poor man. The only obvious opportunity for him to secure such funds would be to indenture himself as a servant (cf. 2 Kings 4:1).

The God of Israel was a redeeming God. He had delivered his servants from bondage in Egypt and did not want them to be in servitude again. The Messiah of Israel, the Servant of the Lord, would proclaim good news to the poor and freedom for captives (Isa. 61:1; Luke 4:18).

As we noted in chapter 7, with regard to the widow who had two sons (2 Kings 4:1–7), the greatest debt that any of us has is the mortgage on our souls. It is a debt we cannot pay. But the good news of the gospel is that there is a redeeming God, and that he will satisfy all claims against us. God shows himself as our Redeemer when he calls the axhead to the surface of the water and frees his servant from the prospect of an enormous debt.

This miracle, like the others in the Elijah and Elisha stories, is redemptive. It points to the future and sets things right. Christ is the guarantee that our debts have been paid (Heb. 7:22). The same God who commanded the waters to float an axhead would later walk on the Sea of Galilee and command the sea (John 6:16–21).

FOR FURTHER REFLECTION

1. This story narrates an incident in which a prophet met God in his work-a-day world, not during a "religious" time in his life. Can you see God's hand in your everyday life, or do you try to restrict him to "special" times and places?
2. The fact that the band of prophets was building larger quarters is testimony to the effectiveness of God's word through the ministries of Elijah and Elisha. Where do you feel the futility of your own labors? Can you see how God redeems them and enables you to work for his glory?
3. God met the needs of the prophet in a moment of crisis, but from his reaction it is not clear that he saw the opportunity for spiritual growth in the crisis. How do you respond in moments of trouble?

4. Americans know what it means to carry too much debt. But the debt of money we may owe as individuals or as a nation is nothing next to the debt and guilt caused by our sins. God has paid that debt and will not let us fall into bondage again. Where in your own life have you felt the cancellation of that debt most keenly?

5. Think of some other Bible stories that we often approach from the what's-here-for-me perspective. For a start, think of the familiar stories of the call of Joshua (Josh. 1) or David and Goliath (1 Sam. 17). How would our understanding of these passages change if we approached them with the question "What do I learn about my Lord?"

B. OPEN OUR EYES, LORD
2 KINGS 6:8–23

Now the king of Aram was at war with Israel. After conferring with his officers, he said, "I will set up my camp in such and such a place."

The man of God sent word to the king of Israel: "Beware of passing that place, because the Arameans are going down there." So the king of Israel checked on the place indicated by the man of God. Time and again Elisha warned the king, so that he was on his guard in such places.

This enraged the king of Aram. He summoned his officers and demanded of them, "Will you not tell me which of us is on the side of the king of Israel?"

"None of us, my lord the king," said one of his officers, "but Elisha, the prophet who is in Israel, tells the king of Israel the very words you speak in your bedroom."

"Go, find out where he is," the king ordered, "so I can send men and capture him." The report came back: "He is in Dothan." Then he sent horses and chariots and a strong force there. They went by night and surrounded the city.

When the servant of the man of God got up and went out early the next morning, an army with horses and chariots had surrounded the city. "Oh, my lord, what shall we do?" the servant asked.

"Don't be afraid," the prophet answered. "Those who are with us are more than those who are with them."

And Elisha prayed, "O LORD, open his eyes so he may see." Then the LORD opened the servant's eyes, and he looked and saw the hills full of horses and chariots of fire all around Elisha.

As the enemy came down toward him, Elisha prayed to the LORD, "Strike these people with blindness." So he struck them with blindness, as Elisha had asked.

Elisha told them, "This is not the road and this is not the city. Follow me, and I will lead you to the man you are looking for." And he led them to Samaria.

After they entered the city, Elisha said, "LORD, open the eyes of these men so they can see." Then the LORD opened their eyes and they looked, and there they were, inside Samaria.

When the king of Israel saw them, he asked Elisha, "Shall I kill them, my father? Shall I kill them?"

"Do not kill them," he answered. "Would you kill men you have captured with your own sword or bow? Set food and water before them so that they may eat and drink and then go back to their master." So he prepared a great feast for them, and after they had finished eating and drinking, he sent them away, and they returned to their master. So the bands from Aram stopped raiding Israel's territory.

The king of Aram was frustrated that Elisha always knew of his plans for the deployment of his troops. His advisors no doubt were exaggerating, but they said that even the king's pillow talk was being reported in Samaria (2 Kings 6:12). This was a new experience for the Aramean king. He served idols—gods that could not see or hear. The mythology of ancient Syria, like that of the Canaanites, depicted gods who could actually control very little, for they were often at war with one another and engaged in their own struggles to survive. They were as subject to contingency and chance as were the mortals who worshiped them. The Aramean king had never dealt with a god from whom nothing is hidden (Heb. 4:13).

The account of the Aramean efforts to besiege Dothan and capture Elisha is a good example of why both Elijah and Elisha could be called "the chariots and horsemen of Israel" (2 Kings 2:12; 13:14). The prophets of Israel often acted in behalf of the nation's warfare. In this brief passage, Elisha is a one-man intelligence operation (6:8–12) and a one-man army (vv. 18–19). The chariots and horses of the divine army accompanied the prophet (v. 17). The same chariot and horses that carried Elijah to heaven (2:11) attended the ministry of his successor.

Have you ever watched a shadow play? The stage action takes place behind a sheet or screen stretched across the front of a stage. Behind the screen and the players, a light casts their shadow toward the screen. The audience in front sees the shadows on the screen.

In some ways, life is a lot like a shadow play. We see all around us the battle between good and evil, right and wrong. But what we see is in so many ways just the battling shadows—the real fight is behind the scenes, where the army of heaven is drawn up against the forces of hell. We often underestimate the reality of the battle behind the scenes and underestimate the power and might of the divine warrior who has fought on our behalf. Elisha's servant was given a glimpse behind the screen (2 Kings 6:17). For him, for a moment, faith became sight. For most of us, however, faith continues to pertain to what we do not see (Heb. 11:1; John 20:29). The battle is nonetheless real. Paul urges us to put on the armor of God and to be strong in his mighty power so that we can resist the devil's schemes (Eph. 6:10–11). "For our struggle is not against flesh and blood, but against the rulers, against the authorities, against the powers of this dark world and against the spiritual forces of evil in the heavenly realms" (v. 12). Let our own prayer be, "Open our eyes, Lord."

When Israel was encamped near the Jordan and on the verge of beginning her warfare for the land that God had promised to her, God gave the nation instructions about holy war (Deut. 7; 20). Paramount among these was, "Do not be fainthearted or afraid. . . . For the LORD your God is the one who goes with you to fight for you against your enemies to give you victory" (20:3–4). God would keep this promise to Israel repeatedly in the nation's history. The God of Israel was a warrior who fought in behalf of his people.

Christian tradition identifies Jesus with the angel of the LORD, the captain of the heavenly army. The child that Isaiah prophesied would be called "the warrior God" (Isa. 9:6).[2] This captain of the heavenly armies, this warrior God, is the one who has fought our battles for us. Just as Elisha enjoyed the unseen presence of the heavenly host, so too the captain of our salvation has promised that he will never leave or abandon us, even to the end of the age (Matt. 28:20). When the difficulties seem insurmountable and the obstacles overwhelming, he is there, and his strength is perfected when we are weak.

This passage not only reminds us that the God of the Old Testament is the same as the God of the New, but also provides some points of contrast. Centuries after Elisha, other men would scheme to capture a prophet from God (Matt. 26:3–5). Just as the enemies of God's people focused on one man in the days of Elisha (2 Kings 6:13), so too the enemy of our souls focused his attack on one man, Jesus. Although he had at his command more than twelve legions of angels (Matt. 26:53), he did not call them to his aid. Rather, he went into combat single-handedly against the forces of evil—and was victorious.

Elisha reminded his servant, "Those who are with us are more than those who are with them" (2 Kings 6:16). John would later remind Christians in the infant church that they would overcome "because the one who is in you is greater than the one who is in the world" (1 John 4:4).

Put yourself for a moment in the place of the Aramean soldiers. Imagine opening your eyes after a period of terrifying, temporary blindness to find yourself surrounded by enemy troops in their own capital city. The siege of Dothan had been reversed, and now the Aramean soldiers were surrounded. Their best hope was probably for no more than a merciful and speedy death (2 Kings 6:21). Instead, they were treated with respect and hospitality; they enjoyed a banquet in the presence of their enemies and were returned to their homeland (v. 23). This event gives us a glimpse of a day when Jew and Gentile will sit down at a banquet together, a banquet spread for all peoples (Isa. 25:6). Similarly, when a Gentile, a Roman centurion, showed great faith, Jesus saw in him an anticipation of a day when "many will come from the east and the west, and will take their places at the feast with Abraham, Isaac and Jacob in the kingdom of heaven" (Matt. 8:11). O Lord, bring us to that banquet, we pray.

We have already described the way in which Matthew draws parallels between Elijah and John the Baptist and between Elisha and Jesus.[3] John the Baptist came in the spirit and power of Elijah. Toward the end of his life, John sent messengers to ask if Jesus was the one who would be his successor. Jesus sent word back to John that he should look at the miracles Jesus was performing (Matt. 11:4–5). John would know that Jesus was his successor, just as Elisha had succeeded Elijah, when he saw Jesus performing the miracles of Elisha. Among those miracles was that the blind receive their sight (2 Kings 6:20; John 9:1–7).

FOR FURTHER REFLECTION

1. Elisha knew the plans made by the Aramean king only because God knew them. God knows even our most private moments. How does this make you feel? Ashamed? Secure?
2. Behind the scenes of this physical world, the angelic armies are deployed against the legions of hell. The world is a battleground for the souls of human beings. Jesus, our divine warrior, has defeated Satan and his forces, but until the last moments of history, Satan rails against God. Where do you see the war between good and evil in our society? In your own life?
3. Sometimes we feel overwhelmed by life. We feel beaten down by people and circumstances. The

prophet said to his servant in the midst of crisis: "Those who are with us are more than those who are with them." Do you recognize this truth in your own life? If not, why not?

4. Elisha returned good for evil to this army that was seeking his life. What does this tell us about God? How are Elisha's actions in this regard reflected in the commands of God?

5. Read Colossians 2:13–15. How does the fact that we now live in the shadow of the Cross and of the Resurrection make a difference in the way you view areas of defeat in your life? Confess your lingering doubts and defeats to our Lord, who is full of compassion and forgiveness.

10

THE POWER OF GOD AND
THE POWER OF THE PROPHET

The king of Israel thought a lot about Elisha the prophet. He was a hard person to ignore. In the next two stories, we read that the king associated Elisha with the power of God. In the first story, the king is angry with Elisha and wants him dead because he knows that his difficulties have originated with Elisha's God. In the second one, he is intrigued by the great wonders that God has worked through Elisha.

A. A SIEGE AND A SON
2 KINGS 6:24–7:2

Some time later, Ben-Hadad king of Aram mobilized his entire army and marched up and laid siege to Samaria. There was a great famine in the city; the siege lasted so long that a donkey's head sold for eighty shekels of silver, and a fourth of a cab of seed pods for five shekels.

As the king of Israel was passing by on the wall, a woman cried to him, "Help me, my lord the king!"

The king replied, "If the LORD does not help you, where can I get help for you? From the threshing floor? From the winepress?" Then he asked her, "What's the matter?"

She answered, "This woman said to me, 'Give up your son so we may eat him today, and tomorrow we'll eat my son.' So we cooked my son and ate him. The next day I said to her, 'Give up your son so we may eat him,' but she had hidden him."

When the king heard the woman's words, he tore his robes. As he went along the wall, the people looked, and there, underneath, he had sackcloth on his body. He said, "May God deal with me, be it ever so severely, if the head of Elisha son of Shaphat remains on his shoulders today!"

Now Elisha was sitting in his house, and the elders were sitting with him. The king sent a messenger ahead, but before he arrived, Elisha said to the elders, "Don't you see how this murderer is sending someone to cut off my head? Look, when the messenger comes, shut the door and hold it shut against him. Is not the sound of his master's footsteps behind him?"

While he was still talking to them, the messenger came down to him. And the king said, "This disaster is from the Lord. Why should I wait for the Lord any longer?"

Elisha said, "Hear the word of the Lord. This is what the Lord says: About this time tomorrow, a seah of flour will sell for a shekel and two seahs of barley for a shekel at the gate of Samaria."

The officer on whose arm the king was leaning said to the man of God, "Look, even if the Lord should open the floodgates of the heavens, could this happen?"

"You will see it with your own eyes," answered Elisha, "but you will not eat any of it!"

The writer of Kings was much concerned to demonstrate the power of the words of the prophets. Repeatedly throughout the book he calls attention to the way in which the words of the prophets came to pass (Deut. 18:21–22; 1 Kings 13:1–2, 5, 21, 26, 32; 15:29; 16:7, 12, 34; 17:16, 24; 22:38; 2 Kings 1:17; 7:1, 17–20; 9:26, 36–37; 10:17; 14:25; 15:12; 23:16; 24:2). Moses was the model prophet and the founder of the prophetic order in Israel (Deut. 18:15, 18). If the words of the prophets came to pass, how much more so the words of Moses! Toward the end of Deuteronomy, there is a chapter cataloging the blessings that would come to Israel if she kept covenant with God (Deut. 28:1–14) and the curses that would come as a consequence of disobedience (vv. 15–68). The writer of Kings takes these curses and shows how they were actually realized in the life of the nation. Moses had warned Israel that if they were a disobedient people, foreign armies would come against them and besiege their cities. He warned them further,

> Because of the suffering that your enemy will inflict on you during the siege, you will eat the fruit of the womb, the flesh of the sons and daughters the LORD your God has given you. Even the most gentle and sensitive man among you will have no compassion on his own brother or the wife he loves or his surviving children, and he will not give to one of them any of the flesh of his children that he is eating. It will be all he has left because of the suffering your enemy will inflict on you during the siege of all your cities. The most gentle and sensitive woman among you—so sensitive and gentle that she would not venture to touch the ground with the sole of her foot—will begrudge the husband she loves and her own son or daughter the afterbirth from her womb and the

children she bears. For she intends to eat them secretly during the siege and in the distress that your enemy will inflict on you in your cities. (Deut. 28:53–57; cf. Lev. 26:29)

This sorry story shows that the words of the great prophet Moses had also come to pass. Judah would have a similar experience when the Babylonians besieged Jerusalem just before it was destroyed (Lam. 4:9–10; Jer. 19:9; Ezek. 5:10).

This passage reminds us of the holiness and justice of God. The One who created us has the right to call us to obedience. He who is without sin holds us to account for our rebellion against him. Because God is just and because he cannot look upon sin, sin results in punishment. The writer of Hebrews would centuries later look at the old covenant and remember that it was binding, and that "every violation and disobedience received its just punishment" (Heb. 2:2). As awful as it may seem to us, the justice of God is not deterred by the awful specter of a mother devouring her child.

The great prophet Isaiah once asked a rhetorical question: "Can a mother forget the baby at her breast?" (Isa. 49:15). The expected answer was, "No, of course she can't." But alas, it was possible. We have seen in our own generation, on the streets of the great cities of industrialized nations, how drugs and substance abuse leave in their wake the neglect, abuse, and abandonment of children.

A human parent may "forget" his or her child and put his or her own needs ahead of the child's needs, even to the point of taking the child's life. But God promised Isaiah that, even though a mother might forget the child that grew in her womb, he would never forget his people (Isa. 49:15). For those in dire straits, he had prepared a banquet. The words of the prophet would come to pass, and the morning would bring plenty and feasting (2 Kings 7:1, 18).

Perhaps the king was blaming Elisha for the siege of Samaria. After all, it was Elisha who instructed the king of Israel not to kill the soldiers of the Aramean army in the immediately preceding story (2 Kings 6:22). But this seems unlikely in light of the fact that "bands from Aram stopped raiding Israel's territory" (v. 23). The text is silent on the point, but a more probable explanation is that the king was angry because Elisha had announced that the siege was an instance of divine judgment. The king typifies the response of our world to the word of a righteous God. It is always a temptation to "shoot the messenger" when he brings bad news (2 Kings 6:31). The history of the prophets in Israel is a history of murder (Matt. 23:29–31, 37). But the same prophet who had announced God's judgment on the city would also announce its salvation and deliverance.

Is it any surprise that our world responded the way it did to that last and greatest prophet, Jesus Christ? The words of Jesus were convicting the generation of his day of sin. Although he would also announce salvation and deliverance, they would rather have him dead than hear the call to repentance.

One cannot leave this passage without hearing the warning it contains about the delusion and transitoriness of riches. One cannot eat silver and gold (2 Kings 6:25). All that people strive for may amount to no more than the head of a dead donkey or a few thimbles-full of dove dung or seed hulls. Wealth cannot save us in our extremity. Of what use is wealth on the day of the Lord? It cannot save us from famine—how can it save us from the wrath of God? But hear instead the word of Israel's God: "Come, all you who are thirsty, come to the waters; and you who have no money, come, buy and eat! Come, buy wine and milk without money and without cost" (Isa. 55:1).

The God whose holiness requires that he punish sin is also a God who is eager to forgive those who seek his mercy. For the repentant he has made abundant provision. Because of the Lord's great love, we are not consumed in his anger; his compassion never fails (Lam. 3:22).

FOR FURTHER REFLECTION

1. The king of Samaria blamed God and Elisha for the disaster that had befallen the kingdom (2 Kings 6:33). He planned to kill Elisha. What should his response have been?
2. God's rule over history is shown in the fulfillment of the words of the prophets. What promises of God bring you comfort in difficult times?
3. The animosity of a wicked world is directed against God and against those who announce his word. Have you had the opportunity to share in the sufferings of Christ (Rom. 8:17–18; Phil. 3:10; 1 Peter 4:13)? When and how—or, why not?
4. The officer of the king doubted the word of the prophet, and his doom was sealed because of it. The Bible is the word of God to us today. What should our attitude toward it be?
5. We looked briefly at the delusion and transitoriness of riches, against which this passage warns. Are there subtle areas in your life where you have begun to believe the lie that there is salvation in earthly wealth? How might you need to change?

B. THE PLIGHT OF THE HOMELESS
2 KINGS 8:1–6

Now Elisha had said to the woman whose son he had restored to life, "Go away with your family and stay for a while wherever you can, because the LORD has decreed a famine in the land that will last seven years." The woman proceeded to do as the man of God said. She and her family went away and stayed in the land of the Philistines seven years.

At the end of the seven years she came back from the land of the Philistines and went to the king to beg for her house and land. The king was talking to Gehazi, the servant of the man of God, and had said, "Tell me about all the great things Elisha has done." Just as Gehazi was telling the king how Elisha had restored the dead to life, the woman whose son Elisha had brought back to life came to beg the king for her house and land.

Gehazi said, "This is the woman, my lord the king, and this is her son whom Elisha restored to life." The king asked the woman about it, and she told him.

Then he assigned an official to her case and said to him, "Give back everything that belonged to her, including all the income from her land from the day she left the country until now."

The first time we met this lady, she was doing quite well, materially speaking. She lacked nothing and had "a home among my own people" (2 Kings 4:13). Her goodness toward God and toward his servant the prophet had brought her a blessing beyond her greatest hopes, a son. When that child's life was threatened, she had once again been the object of divine favor, and the child's life was restored (2 Kings 4:32–37). Life could scarcely have been better.

But once again her fortunes turned. She lost that home among her own people. Like Naomi and Elimelech in the book of Ruth, she had been forced by a famine to leave the land and seek greener pastures. She who had earlier in her life had little reason to fear creditors had now lost her land, or perhaps it had been confiscated by the king (cf. 1 Kings 21:16). Ironically, her problem had arisen in part because she had followed the prophet's advice to leave the land.

Our God does not abandon us. Heeding his word will not result in loss. Jesus himself would later enunciate this principle (Matt. 10:40–42).

> He who receives you receives me, and he who receives me receives the one who sent me. Anyone who receives a prophet because he is a prophet will receive a prophet's reward, and anyone who receives a righteous man because he is a righteous man will receive a righteous man's reward. And if anyone gives even a cup of cold water to one of these little ones because he is my disciple, I tell you the truth, he will certainly not lose his reward.

He also said, "Everyone who has left houses or brothers or sisters or father or mother or children or fields for my sake will receive a hundred times as much and will inherit eternal life" (Matt. 19:29).

God provides us with an inheritance as part of our redemption, and he maintains that inheritance for us. This woman's life had been one of obedience to God's commands as given through the prophet. God would not abandon her now. He worked in the heart of the king to see that her inheritance was restored to her. The widow recovered her inheritance and her home. Jesus, in his redeeming of us, has not only secured our inheritance for us, but has gone before us to prepare for us a home, that where he is, we may be also (John 14:1–3).

Remember that the book of Kings was written to exiles living in the Babylonian captivity. They too had been driven from the land they loved, the land that was their inheritance and the fruit of their redemption. Here was a story that spoke powerfully to a community of exiles. It was a reminder of the faithfulness of God. It gave reason to hope that they too could return to their lands. It was an expression of faith that they also would know the grace of God through his preserving of their inheritance for them (cf. Ezek. 11:14–15).

The passage speaks with the same power to the church, that body of aliens and strangers, sojourners and exiles, who are looking for the city whose builder and maker is God. The God who redeemed us and provided us with an inheritance will not lose us during our sojourn. In Christ he has given us an inheritance far greater than a few acres of rocky soil in ancient Palestine. He has made us joint heirs with Jesus, our older brother (Rom. 8:15–17). Peter wrote to the church, consisting of "God's elect, strangers in the world, scattered throughout" many lands (1 Peter 1:1). Peter reminded this church that God has given us an inheritance "kept in heaven for you, who through faith are shielded by God's power until the coming of the salvation that is ready to be revealed in the last time" (vv. 4–5).

Nothing is said in this passage about Gehazi's leprosy. It is not likely that he had recovered (2 Kings 5:27). Elisha had been salt in the earth. Even when he was not personally present, the power of his righteous life lived on in the recitation of his deeds and brought blessing to others. How much more is this true of that One who is greater than Elisha! The proclamation of the saving deeds of Jesus continues to bring justice and salvation throughout the earth. That power is there even when the proclamation comes from the mouth of lepers like us.

One can but marvel at the divine providence that brought the woman before the king at precisely the right moment. Had it been a day or an hour earlier, her request would probably not have been granted. Think of how the woman probably fretted and worried before going to her audience with the king. But God knew before she went what she needed (Matt. 6:8, 28–34). So much of life is wasted with worry when our heavenly Father knows what we need. The course of our life, and indeed of history itself, in all its details, is within his hand. He turns the king's heart as he pleases (Prov. 21:1).

FOR FURTHER REFLECTION

1. We meet this woman from Shunem in a variety of circumstances. First she is wealthy and living well in her home; then she is the mother of a long-awaited son. Now we see her driven from her home by famine. The fact that life is easy right now does not mean that it always will be. But the dark and hard times are just as much under God's control; they are just as much an opportunity for God to reveal his power. Can you recall instances when the times were dark and you experienced the grace and goodness of God?

2. Think of the timing in 2 Kings 8:4–5. God can use seemingly insignificant events, like a simple conversation, to turn the course of events. Can you recall a simple, unplanned event that significantly changed your life? Can you see the providential care of God behind such events?

3. Famine, homelessness, and hunger are enormous problems in our own day. How can you bring glory to God in these areas?

4. Are you mindful of the home that Jesus has prepared for you, pilgrim? All that we have in this life

we can lose—but no one can take that home from us. How should this fact affect our daily lives?

5. So much of our effort is spent figuring out how we might like events to transpire, only to plunge us into worry and disarray when things go awry. Think about your own life and the worries you carry with you. Remind yourself again of your Father's providence and goodness clearly demonstrated in this passage, so that you might have the peace of a beloved child.

I I

THE DEATH OF ELISHA

Two stories end the account of Elisha, God's servant. These accounts are set during the time of his final illness and death. Indeed, the last story shows that God's power in the prophet transcends even his death.

A. ARROWS AND ERRORS
2 KINGS 13:10–19

In the thirty-seventh year of Joash king of Judah, Jehoash son of Jehoahaz became king of Israel in Samaria, and he reigned sixteen years. He did evil in the eyes of the LORD and did not turn away from any of the sins of Jeroboam son of Nebat, which he had caused Israel to commit; he continued in them.

As for the other events of the reign of Jehoash, all he did and his achievements, including his war against Amaziah king of Judah, are they not written in the book of the annals of the kings of Israel? Jehoash rested with his fathers, and Jeroboam succeeded him on the throne. Jehoash was buried in Samaria with the kings of Israel.

Now Elisha was suffering from the illness from which he died. Jehoash king of Israel went down to see him and wept over him. "My father! My father!" he cried. "The chariots and horsemen of Israel!"

Elisha said, "Get a bow and some arrows," and he did so. "Take the bow in your hands," he said to the king of Israel. When he had taken it, Elisha put his hands on the king's hands.

"Open the east window," he said, and he opened it. "Shoot!" Elisha said, and he shot. "The LORD's arrow of victory, the arrow of victory over Aram!" Elisha declared. "You will completely destroy the Arameans at Aphek."

Then he said, "Take the arrows," and the king took them. Elisha told him, "Strike the ground." He struck it three times and stopped. The man of God was angry with him and said, "You should have struck the ground five or six times; then you would have defeated Aram and completely destroyed it. But now you will defeat it only three times."

The prophets had a prominent role to play in Israel's warfare. They delivered God's word to kings regarding the outcome and conduct of battle. The stories about Elijah and Elisha often record the involvement of these prophets in military matters (1 Kings 20; 2 Kings 3; 6:8–7:20; 8:7–15; cf. 1 Kings 21). On one occasion, Elisha told Hazael that he would soon become king of Aram, and prophesied that he would do great harm to Israel (2 Kings 8:12–13). The present chapter records the fulfillment of Elisha's prophecy; it begins by recounting how severely Hazael was oppressing Israel (2 Kings 13:4). Israel had sunk to its lowest point, both in political power and in territorial extent. Hazael had left Jehoahaz with only enough chariots and soldiers to have a nice little parade (v. 7).

God glorifies himself in human weakness. He did not choose as his people the strongest nation on earth or those who were intrinsically the most noble (Deut. 7:6–7; Isa. 41:14). It is precisely when we are at our weakest that the surpassing greatness of God's power to save is most clear (1 Cor. 1:25, 27; 2 Cor. 12:9–10; 13:4, 9). God is the same in both Testaments. His character has not changed.

The Arameans were the principal political foe of the northern kingdom through most of its history. It is fitting that the prophet should announce the end of this traditional conflict at the end of his own life (2 Kings 13:17). The king describes the prophet's worth to the kingdom in a metaphor, calling him "the chariots and horsemen of Israel" (cf. 2 Kings 2:12). Although the prophet would die, God was still the divine warrior. He would fight to save and deliver Israel, and he could both declare and effect the outcome of the battle.

Arrows were widely used in divination rituals and symbolism among the Egyptians and the Mesopotamians, especially with regard to warfare. Wall murals depict pharaohs firing arrows in the direction of the four cardinal compass points as a means of signifying their universal dominion.[1] Ezekiel describes Nebuchadnezzar's use of arrows in divination as his forces approach Israel (Ezek. 21:21).

In passages depicting God as the divine warrior, bow and arrows are often the weapon of choice (Pss. 18:14; 45:5; 64:7; Lam. 3:12–13; Hab. 3:9–11; Zech. 9:14). Elisha's gesture of placing his hands on the hands of Jehoash probably had the same significance as "laying on of hands" does in many biblical passages: it represented a conveying of grace and blessing, power and authority. Elisha, "the chariots and horsemen of Israel" and spokesman for the divine warrior, conveyed the power of his Lord to the king for victory over Aram. The nation would go from its lowest point to a resurgence and revival under the last king of Jehu's dynasty, Jeroboam II (2 Kings 14:23–25).

The Bible is often silent precisely at points where the reader wishes more had been said. Why was the king so timid in striking the ground with the arrows? In the first part of the symbolic action, he had already learned that the arrow represented victory over Aram—why not a bit more vigor in the second part of the symbol? The text simply does not tell us, and readers are left to their own impressions of the psychological state of the king. Perhaps he wasn't convinced, or he doubted, or he lacked faith, or he found the whole procedure curious. It is not possible to know.

God's promises always require faith. They require the wholehearted response and endorsement of our souls. It is by faith that the weak become powerful in battle and rout foreign armies (Heb. 11:34).

This story must have spoken powerfully to the original audience of the book of Kings as they lived in exile. At that time in history, Israel was again at her weakest, and foreign oppressors had left her little. The God of Elisha had brought deliverance for Jehoahaz and Jehoash (2 Kings 13:5, 17), and under Jeroboam II would restore the nation to its Solomonic borders (14:25). He could show himself strong in the face of the exiles' weakness. The divine warrior could again fight for his people.

FOR FURTHER REFLECTION

1. It is interesting to see the way in which God's promises that Aram would be defeated were tied to Jehoash's enthusiasm for the task. Jehoash

knew that Aram had often defeated Israel. Do you recall times when you felt too defeated or discouraged to show much enthusiasm for the promises of God? What are your responsibilities in the face of his promises? Remember, God feeds the birds, but does not throw the food into the nest.

2. In this incident, Israel was at its weakest point when God gave victory over its most persistent enemy. What does this tell us about God? About the victory that Jesus won at the Cross?

3. The prophet used divination to communicate with the king. Does that seem appropriate to you? Are there any other places where God's people use divination?

4. Although Elisha had worked miracles of healing and had even raised the dead to life, he was himself suffering a terminal illness (13:14). God had glorified himself in the prophet's life and would now glorify himself in the prophet's death. How do we pray in such circumstances?

5. Do you remember the phrase "the chariots and horsemen of Israel" and its significance? If not, go back to the discussion of 2 Kings 2:1–18 and review.

B. CAN THESE BONES LIVE?
2 KINGS 13:20–21

Elisha died and was buried.

Now Moabite raiders used to enter the country every spring. Once while some Israelites were burying a man, suddenly they saw a band of raiders; so they threw the man's body into Elisha's tomb. When the body touched Elisha's bones, the man came to life and stood up on his feet.

This is the sort of story that provokes the mockery and skepticism of many who read the Bible. It is so easily dismissed as one more example of the kind of ancient myth that grew up around a venerated figure like Elisha. Others are not quite as skeptical, but still feel obliged to seek some sort of naturalistic explanation for the event: "The man was not really dead, but was in a coma. He was jarred back to consciousness when he was dropped into the tomb. It was a miracle all right, but not one that should tax our ability to believe."

There is no real question about what the author of the story intended, however. The man whose corpse was tossed into Elisha's tomb was not comatose, drunk, or in a deep sleep—he was dead. Keep in mind the nature of miracle in the Bible: miracle is redemptive, and it points forward to the restoration of all things. In this little story, we have a glimpse of what redemption will ultimately mean—victory over death and restoration to life. It is a tiny vignette of a day when death itself will be destroyed, a glimpse of a city in which there "will be no more death or mourning" (Rev. 21:4).

It is fitting that the last two stories pertaining to Elisha report his role in the destruction of enemies—both the great national enemy at the time, Aram (2 Kings 13:10–19), and the greatest personal enemy, death (vv. 20–21). The defeat of that great national enemy was a foretaste of the nation's renewal during the reign of Jeroboam II (14:25). Similarly, the victory over death was a foretaste of a yet greater victory over the grave.

Ezekiel was preaching to the same community of exiles for whom the book of Kings was written, and he combined both images. He described victory over another great national enemy and the renewal of the nation as a restoration to life from the dead (Ezek. 37:1–14). The breath and spirit of God, infused into dry bones, was symbolic of the restoration of God's people to the inheritance he had promised to them.

It was many centuries later than both the date of these events and the date when the book of Kings was written that Israel once again faced a great national enemy. Jerusalem again faced divine judgment through destruction by a foreign power—Rome (A.D. 70). A few decades earlier, a prophet, a man who embodied faithful Israel and had kept God's law perfectly, underwent divine judgment for sin. He died and was exiled from his heavenly father (Matt. 27:46), but then enjoyed victory over death and a restoration to life as the founder of a new Israel, a new people of God, the church. Just as in Elisha's day and in Ezekiel's day, new life for the nation would begin where there was only death and defeat. In the new covenant, life for the community flows from the resurrection of Jesus, from his destruction of that last and greatest enemy.

This miracle was God's own seal of approval on the ministry of Elisha. In time, one greater than Elisha would come, and God would set his approval on him, declaring him to be the Son of God with power by his resurrection from the dead (Rom. 1:4). Others in the narrative of Elijah and Elisha had known restoration to life through the prophets' identification with them in death (1 Kings 17:19–21; 2 Kings 4:34–37). It should come as no surprise that at the hour of the death of the Son of God, "tombs broke open and the bodies of many holy people who had died were raised to life" (Matt. 27:52).

It is sad that many have misread this passage and fallen into confusion as a result. Perhaps more than any other biblical passage, this short story is responsible for the largely Roman Catholic practice of venerating the relics of the saints. It is as if the bones and the other fragments and detritus of their lives had some inherently magical power. But make no mistake about it: it was not the dead corpse of Elisha that brought life back to this man. It was the command of the living God. It was not magic, but the magnificent grace and power of the God who both gives and takes life.

FOR FURTHER REFLECTION

1. This episode concerns death—not just the death of Elisha, but the death of an unnamed man. Death horrifies us. What lessons about God's relationship with death do we learn from this story?
2. Many of us go through life in a nearly comatose fashion, fearful of failure, disapproval, harm, and death. What does this story tell us about our fears?
3. God's seal of approval on the life of Elisha was that even in death he was involved in bringing life to an unnamed man. God's seal of approval on Elisha's greater successor was similar: Jesus was one "who through the Spirit of holiness was declared with power to be the Son of God by his resurrection from the dead" (Rom. 1:4). The resurrection of the body is not just some idle theological speculation. It's about your body, which, no matter how long it rests in the grave, will one day be restored to life. What does it mean to have the life-giving Jesus touch your life?
4. The hope of the resurrection is not just a vague hope for the future. It has consequences for our lives today. Because we are risen with Christ, our hearts are set on things above. How does this knowledge of your resurrection affect the way you live now?
5. In this story, Elisha's bones seem to have some kind of miraculous healing power. Where is the real power in the story?

NOTES

CHAPTER ONE

1   "Yahweh" is the way the name of God was most probably pronounced. In older Christian tradition, the name was often pronounced "Jehovah," although this pronunciation was never actually used in the biblical period itself. Most English translations of the Bible represent this name as "LORD" (using small capitals).

2   See D. G. Bostock, "Jesus as the New Elisha," *Expository Times* 92 (1980): 39–41, and T. L. Brodie, "Jesus as the New Elisha: Cracking the Code," *Expository Times* 93 (1981): 39–42.

CHAPTER TWO

1   I Aqht, I:42–46; cf. L. Bronner, *The Stories of Elijah and Elisha* (Leiden: Brill, 1968), 68.

2   C. H. Gordon, *Ugaritic Textbook* (Rome: Pontifical Biblical Institute, 1965), text 67, V:6–8.

3   Gordon, *Ugaritic Textbook,* text 49, III:4–9; cf. Bronner, *The Stories of Elijah and Elisha,* 71.

CHAPTER FOUR

1   The three Hebrew words translated "a still small voice" in 1 Kings 19:12 (KJV, RSV) occur together only here. They have been the subject of much debate. Many scholars propose an almost opposite meaning and translate "a roaring and thunderous voice." On this approach, God reveals himself as he did at Sinai, including the loud and terrifying sound and voice (Ex. 19:16, 19). See J. Lust, "A Gentle Breeze or a Roaring Thunderous Sound?" *Vetus Testamentum* 25 (1975): 110–15.

2   For a fuller discussion of these passages, see R. Dillard, "Joel," in *The Minor Prophets: An Exegetical and Expository Commentary,* ed. Thomas E. McComiskey (Grand Rapids: Baker, 1992).

3   S. DeVries, *1 Kings,* Word Biblical Commentary (Waco, Tex.: Word, 1985), 240.

4   Jesus often used strong hyperbole to make his point. Compare Matt. 5:29–30; 19:24. The Jesus who cared for his own mother at the foot of the cross (John 19:25–27) is not urging that his disciples fail to "honor your father and your mother" (Ex. 20:12). His point is that since he is greater than Elijah, his demands for greater devotion are legitimate. Christianity is not a cruel faith, but commitment to Christ will surely entail some sacrifice.

CHAPTER SIX

1   See T. Longman III and D. Reid, *God Is a Warrior* (Grand Rapids: Zondervan, 1995).

2   For more, see D. B. Allender and T. Longman III, *Bold Love* (Colorado Springs: NavPress, 1992).

3   See chapter 1, "Christians and the Old Testament," particularly the last section in the chapter, "(3) Later biblical interpretation."

4   See L. Bronner, *The Stories of Elijah and Elisha* (Leiden: Brill, 1968), 127–33.

CHAPTER SEVEN

1   How quickly the tables can turn! See 2 Kings 8:1–6.

CHAPTER EIGHT

1   It is important to note that the disease called "leprosy" in most English Bibles was not the same as Hansen's disease, which we designate today as leprosy. "Leprosy" in the biblical period was more probably a fungal disease of the skin; its symptoms resembled psoriasis. Those who are more interested in this subject should read S. G. Browne, *Leprosy in the Bible* (London: Christian Medical Society, 1970), or E. V. Hulse, "The Nature of Biblical 'Leprosy' and the Use of Alternative Medical Terms in Modern Translations of the Bible," *Palestinian Exploration Quarterly* 107 (1975): 87–105.

CHAPTER NINE

1 See page 86 above.
2 This phrase is commonly translated "Mighty God" (NIV). The Hebrew is literally "God of a warrior" (*'el gibbor*), a construction in which the second noun is often adjectival to the first. The other phrases in Isa. 9:6 are also similar in structure: "wonder of a counselor," "prince of peace," "father of continuous existence."
3 See chapter 1, the final section, *"3 Later biblical interpretation."*

CHAPTER ELEVEN

1 A discussion of these representations and similar portrayals is found in B. Couroyer, "A propos de II Rois XIII, 14–19," *Studium Biblicanum Franciscanum* 30 (1980): 177–96.

FOR FURTHER READING

Allender, D. B., and T. Longman III. *Bold Love.* Colorado Springs: NavPress, 1992.

Battenfield, J. R. "YHWH's Refutation of the Baal Myth Through the Actions of Elijah and Elisha." In *Israel's Apostasy and Restoration.* Edited by A. Gileadi, 19–37. Grand Rapids: Baker, 1988.

Blomberg, C. L. "Elijah, Election, and the Use of Malachi in the New Testament." *Criswell Theological Review* 2 (1987): 99–117.

Bronner, L. *The Stories of Elijah and Elisha.* Leiden: Brill, 1968.

Brower, K. "Elijah in the Markan Passion Narrative." *Journal for the Study of the New Testament* 18 (1983): 85–101.

Childs, B. S. "On Reading the Elijah Narratives." *Interpretation* 34 (1980): 128–37.

Cohn, R. "The Literary Logic of 1 Kings 17–19." *Journal of Biblical Literature* 101 (1982): 333–50.

DeVries, S. *1 Kings.* Word Biblical Commentary. Waco, Tex.: Word, 1985.

Dumbrell, W. J. "What Are You Doing Here? Elijah at Horeb." *Crux* 22 (1986): 12–19.

Evans, C. A. "Luke's Use of the Elijah/Elisha Narratives and the Ethic of Election." *Journal of Biblical Literature* 106 (1987): 75–83.

Gray, J. *I and II Kings.* 2d rev. ed. Philadelphia: Westminster, 1970.

Hobbs, T. R. *2 Kings.* Word Biblical Commentary. Waco, Tex.: Word, 1985.

Jones, G. H. *1 and 2 Kings.* New Century Bible Commentary. 2 vols. Grand Rapids: Eerdmans, 1984.

Kaiser, W. C., Jr. "The Promise of the Arrival of Elijah in Malachi and the Gospels." *Grace Theological Journal* 32 (1982): 221–33.

Longman, T., III, and D. Reid. *God Is a Warrior.* Grand Rapids: Zondervan, 1995.

Miller, R. J. "Elijah, John, and Jesus in the Gospel of Luke." *New Testament Studies* 34 (1988): 611–22.

Ottosson, M. "The Prophet Elijah's Visit to Zarephath." In *In the Shelter of Elyon,* ed. W. Barrick and J. Spencer, 185–98. Journal for the Study of the Old Testament, Supplement Series, 31. Sheffield: JSOT Press, 1984.

Rongen, G. Van. *Elisha the Prophet.* Kelmscott, Australia: Pro Ecclesia, 1988.

Stewart, A. *A Prophet of Grace: An Expository and Devotional Study of the Life of Elisha.* Edinburgh: Henderson, 1925.

Van't Veer, M. B. *My God Is Yahweh: Elijah and Elisha in an Age of Apostasy.* Translated by T. Plantinga. St. Catharines, Ontario: Paideia, 1980.

Wallace, R. S. *Elijah and Elisha.* Grand Rapids: Eerdmans, 1957.

INDEX OF SCRIPTURE

21:21—149
22:7—95
23:48—123
27:17—24
33:11—72
37:1-14—152
47:1-12—90
47:12—26, 96

Daniel
2:28-30—71
2:34—59
4:34-35—77
7:10—86
7:13-14—84

Hosea
2:2-13—6
2:5—6
10:4—107

Joel
2:5—84
2:28—60
2:28-29—61
3:18—26, 96

Amos
8:11—21
9:13-15—26, 96

Jonah
2:3-5—118
2:3-6—86

Habakkuk
3:8—84
3:9-11—149

Zechariah
3:9—59
3:10—26, 96
4:7—59

6:1-2—84
7:10—95
7:12—60
9:14—149

Malachi
3:5—95
4:4-5—13
4:5—10, 12
4:5-6—9
4:6—11

Matthew
3:3—12
3:4—10, 87
3:11—79
3:16—11
3:16-17—87
3:17—11
4:2—55
4:15—25
4:21-22—62
5:29-30—156
5:43-45—117
5:45—20, 46
6:8—144
6:13—39
6:19-20—70
6:20-21—70
6:24—38, 46
6:25—139
6:28-34—144
6:33—38, 95
8:11—132
9:9—62
10:25—77
10:28—38
10:32-33—38
10:40—101
10:40-42—142
10:41—101
10:42—108
11:2-5—12

11:4-5—132
11:14—10
12:24—77
12:27—77
13:24-30—54
14:1-12—57
14:3-12—10
14:13-21—109
15:32-39—109
17:1-13—55
17:2-3—11
17:3-4—13
17:12—10
18:23-25—96
18:35—96
19:24—156
19:29—142
20:19—91
21:33-41—39
23:29-31—139
23:37—139
24:30—84
26—20
26:3-5—131
26:53—131
26:59-66—71
26:64—84
27:29—91
27:31—91
27:40—92
27:41—91
27:42—92
27:44—92
27:46—57, 153
27:47-49—20, 79
27:52—153
28:20—130

Mark
3:22—77
6:17-18—38
6:32-44—109
6:37—109